Table of Contents

From the President . . . .
Gardens for All Statement of Purpose 3
THE BIG THREE 5
  Lettuce 5
  Spinach 6
  Chard 7
GETTING READY 8
  Planning on Paper 8
  Planning Tips 8
  Rich Soil: Greens Love It 9
  About pH 9
  A Scratch in Time Saves 9
  Fertilizer 10
PLANTING 10
  Wide Rows — Greener Garden 10
  Time to Plant — Wide Rows 11
  Single Row Planting 12
  Double or Triple Rows 12
  To Win — Thin! 12
THE WORLD OF GREENS 13
Two for the Price of One 13
Cabbage Family Greens 14
  Mustard 14
  Collards — Headless Cabbages 14
  Kale 15
  Cabbage Family Pests 15
GROWING 16
  Weeds and Cultivation 16
  Water 16
  Diseases 17
  Pests 17
  Curing Lettuce Problems 18
Tips For Growing Head Lettuce 18
Booster Shot 20
Lettuce Tips for Roadside Stand 20
Heading Into Fall 21
AND STILL MORE GREENS 21
  Endive 21
  Chicory 21
  Winter Chicory or French Endive 21
  Rocket 22
  Dandelion 22
  Corn Salad 23
  Celtuce 23
  Curlicress or Pepper Grass 23
  Watercress 23
  Upland Cress 24
  Celery 24
HARVESTING 26
  Easy Cold Frames 26
FAVORITE RECIPES 27
CANNING GREENS 27
FREEZING GREENS 27

From the President

Greens are grown by most of our members and for good reasons:
- home grown salad greens taste better
- greens grow quickly and everywhere
- greens can be harvested on a continual basis, starting early and ending late
- greens provide a broad range of nutritional value

Given the current cost of food, it's difficult not to mention the economic benefits of gardening as we christen this book on greens.

In recent years, the price of a head of lettuce has varied from about 30¢ a head all the way to more than $2. Think of it . . . a small, inexpensive packet of seeds, a small patch of ground, flower bed, or walkway and the result — anywhere from 10 to 30 home-grown terrific heads of lettuce.

Some 50 years ago, Dick Raymond gardened to help his parents feed their large family. Dick still gardens today to help feed his own family and he'll be the first to tell you that it's not always easy to save huge sums of money by gardening. But Dick's quick to agree with us on the subject of salad greens.

"I still get a queasy feeling in my stomach" he says, "when I see someone shelling out dollar bills for lettuce."

We at Gardens for All are happy to bring you this timely book, one in an eleven book series, for your gardening library . . . and we hope you never again have to empty your wallet on supermarket greens.

Sincerely,

Jack Robinson

About Gardens for All

Our statement of purpose

Gardens for All, The National Association for Gardening, a non-profit organization established in 1972, is dedicated to encouraging more successful food gardening by people of all ages at home, in community groups, and in institutions because we believe gardening benefits our health, spirit, and environment.

Gardens for All encourages successful home and community food gardening nationwide through:

— *Magazines, Books.* GFA's informal, widely-read national publication, *The Gardens for All Newsmagazine,* how-to books, community gardening manuals, and gardening information service each suggest imaginative, practical, better ways to garden, and bring successful gardening tips and techniques to the attention of gardeners and potential gardeners across the United States.

— *Community Garden Programs.* GFA's community gardening programs encourage gardening for groups without land, the disabled, the elderly, school, church, and youth groups, and those in institutions such as prisons, hospitals, and low-income housing projects. From its broad range of community and institutional experiences, GFA is publishing a manual series, emphasizing steady improvement of productive land, a diminishing resource.

— *Testing Tools and Products.* GFA provides information to members on the best gardening tools, products, techniques, and systems to make gardening easier and more productive.

— *Clearinghouse.* Most of all, Gardens for All connects gardeners with other gardeners. We are the most comprehensive clearinghouse for home and community food gardening information anywhere.

For more information about Gardens for All, please write us at:

Gardens for All
180 Flynn Avenue
Burlington, Vermont 05401

Hello Gardening Friends —

The folks who come by to see my garden each summer always stop short when they catch sight of my wide rows of salad crops. The lush growth and multi-colored foliage really is something to behold! The pale green leaves of Oak Leaf and Black Seeded Simpson lettuce spills into the deep red of Ruby Swiss chard, and this in turn gives way to the dark rich green of Winter Bloomsdale spinach, followed by husky stalks of celery. It's the picture of garden vitality — all in just a small section of garden soil!

The greens harvest is just as appealing to the tastebuds as the growing crops are to the eye. Huge bowls of crisp summer salads are standard fare at the Raymond house, but Jan also cooks up greens casseroles, spicy soups and stews as well as fancy quiches. She's included a mouth-watering array of her best recipes in this book.

If you've been dreaming of a 'greener' garden, you're about to discover that these crops are simple to grow — outdoors, indoors, in the spring or fall or even 12 months a year. And it's our pleasure to tell you the whole story. From the tricks of raising head lettuce to the tips on freezing spinach, we hope you'll use this book over and over, and enjoy a bountiful harvest as well.

Dick Raymond

What Greens Need

The green gardening season at our place starts as soon as the sun and rising temperatures start to warm up the top few inches of soil in early spring. We don't delay our first garden chores — we've planted early crops of lettuce, spinach and chard in April with snow still covering the ground in the shady woods near the garden.

You see, most green crops thrive in cool spring and fall temperatures (50-60°F). Just compare the crisp, flavorful lettuce leaves harvested in spring with the often flaggy, bitter leaves of a summer cutting and you'll agree. A few greens can handle summer heat, but most of them prefer the spring and fall climate.

A steady flow of moisture and nutrients is important for good greens growth. And for some greens, these supplies have to be near the surface. The roots of lettuce, for example, are rather limited — they're close to the surface. They don't grow deep in the soil to search out food and water. If you've gardened in dry times, you know lettuce is not too drought-resistant. Big-leaved plants give off a lot of moisture. When it's dry, they get very thirsty!

Leafy crops need plenty of nitrogen, too. That's the key element in the good growth of leaves and it influences the crispness and quality of leafy crops, too.

A lot of heat is what most greens don't need. Spinach, for example, will quickly develop a seedstalk and start to stretch upward when it gets too warm. This is known as going to seed or "bolting." When it happens, spinach leaves start to lose some of their flavor. A long hot spell can spoil heads of iceberg-type lettuce, too. The heat loosens the leaves of the head, and they get soft and sometimes bitter. If you can shade some of these crops as hot weather approaches, you can often keep the harvest going pretty well.

But, basically, greens are straightforward to grow — so, let's get started!

THE BIG THREE
Lettuce

"Lettuce" is synonymous with "salad" for people all over the world. It's by far the world's most popular salad plant and has been cultivated for more than 2,000 years. Ancient records note that lettuce was served at the royal table of Persian kings as early as 550 B.C. And today you rarely see a home garden without some kind of lettuce growing in it.

The unitiated may think, "Lettuce is lettuce." Not so! There are wonderful varieties. Each has a distinct flavor, texture and color, so you can have remarkably different salads just by varying the lettuces you use. Here's a rundown of what you can expect in the lettuce department:

With the way **head lettuce** prices have jumped around the last couple of seasons, head lettuce is always in my garden plan. Some people refer to all head lettuce as "crisphead" or "iceberg" lettuce. Crisphead is probably a better catch-all term, since technically iceberg is just one variety of head let-

tuce. Early each season I put out several dozen young plants that I've started inside. Starting the plants early indoors enables us to get a good harvest of firm, crispy-leaved heads before the summer heat stops production.

Great Lakes, Iceberg and **Ithaca** are head lettuce varieties which have been good in my garden. Gardeners in the South may want to try varieties which do better when the weather gets hot, such as **Premier Great Lakes.**

Butterhead or **'loosehead' lettuce** plants form a head, but the leaves don't wrap themselves tightly together. They're more open and greener. My favorite loosehead variety is **Dark Green Boston.** I devote quite a bit of space to it each year, planting the seeds as early as peas and growing them in wide rows 15 or 16 inches across. You can harvest many tasty heads from a row 6 to 10 feet long.

The taste and crispness of Dark Green Boston is terrific. The leaves are crunchier than leaf lettuce. The outer leaves of the head are dark green, and the

inner leaves are lighter-colored, sometimes even whitish.

Buttercrunch and **Bibb** are two other good and popular loosehead varieties. You can harvest some loosehead plants before they form a head to have an early harvest of tasty leaves. A second crop will follow. To harvest, simply take a knife and cut the entire plant off about 1 inch above the ground.

Leaf lettuce doesn't form a head at all — it grows up and out. It's very easy to plant and will grow anywhere, almost anytime. Make regular plantings every few weeks over the entire season, starting as soon as you can work the soil in the spring. That way you always have lettuce that is young and fresh. Never give the crop time to get old, tough and bitter — harvest at the peak of freshness and taste.

The flavor of **Black Seeded Simpson** is probably my favorite. I like **Oak Leaf,** too, because it is ready to eat so quickly. After harvesting Oak Leaf by cutting the plants back to an inch above ground, it'll come right back. Sometimes you can get 3 or 4 good-tasting cuttings from one planting of Oak Leaf or any other kind of leaf lettuce, too.

Make sure to include some **Ruby Leaf** lettuce, too. It adds great color and taste to a salad, and looks beautiful in the garden.

Cos or **Romaine lettuce** always has a spot in the garden. Plant the seeds very early like other varieties, but plant them a little thicker because Romaine lettuce doesn't germinate as well as other kinds of lettuce.

The plants produce a tall head — 10 inches or more — of dark green leaves and close up firmly. The tight, inner leaves are especially tasty in tossed salads because they often have a pleasant, mild taste.

Romaine lettuce takes a little while longer to form a full-grown head — about 70 or 80 days. You can harvest them earlier, of course, just like loosehead lettuce. Cut it before it forms a head, and it will come back to give you an additional harvest.

Parris Island Cos is the Romaine variety we grow most often.

Spinach

Spinach is the most versatile green because it fits into almost any part of the menu. But if you want to feature spinach as the main vegetable of a meal, you need to plant a lot to have enough to go around.

The leaves of a robust spinach plant are large, and if you've ever grown spinach, you know it doesn't take many leaves to fill a basket. But, when you cook them, they really wilt, and a lot turns to a little.

To get a lot of spinach from a small space, I plant it in wide rows, perhaps 15 to 20 inches across. Because spinach thrives in cool weather, I plant early in spring and again in late summer for a fall harvest.

I like to see gardeners expand their spinach production because it's one of the most nutritious greens. Raw spinach is very high in vitamin A and tasty in salads. Very little of this important vitamin is lost in canning or freezing, so you can pack a lot of nutrition in your canning jars or freezer cartons. Spinach has a lot of vitamins C and E plus others, too.

We used to think the iron content of spinach was its leading asset. Remember how "Popeye the Sailor Man" created instant muscle by downing a serving of spinach? Well, nutritionists have now shown that it is impossible for the body to use all the iron in spinach. The iron is present in a form the body can't assimilate. Sorry about that, Popeye.

Don't be afraid to start your spinach plantings early. Otherwise, early summer heat may send your plants into the seed stage before your harvest — you'll know you waited too late to plant.

There are two varieties that I often plant: **Avon Hybrid,** which has large, somewhat crinkled leaves; and **Bloomsdale Long-Standing,** with very large and crinkled leaves. The big leaves are easiest to cook and freeze. Bloomsdale Long-Standing has a tendency to bolt, though, if not harvested properly.

Another good variety is **Winter Bloomsdale.** It's a nice fall-harvested spinach; and many gardeners, especially those in the South where winters are mild, plant it in the fall to harvest through the cool winter months and early spring.

And then there's **New Zealand Spinach.** I wish this spinach substitute tasted as good as spinach. The first year I grew it I ate some leaves raw: Ugh! Don't use them in a salad. To approach the taste of spinach they must be cooked.

People grow New Zealand Spinach because it produces in hot weather when spinach won't. It's not a true spinach, though. It's a member of a different plant family and native to New Zealand. It hasn't ever gone to seed in my garden, so we use it for spinach-like flavor in cooked dishes when our true spinach has gone by.

I know one man with a small garden, though, who has kicked the regular spinach off his crop list in favor of the New Zealand type. In his small space, he wants a crop that will give him a season-long harvest.

Some gardeners advise soaking the very hard New Zealand seeds for a day before planting, to help germination. But you can have good stands of this green without soaking; just plant it early in the season when the soil is quite moist.

The plants grow a foot or two high. To harvest, pick off the leaves you need — don't cut the plant back and don't pick off the top.

Chard

As a gardener I like chard because it'll grow in cool *and* warm weather. This ability to grow through the summer sets it apart from most greens, and should put chard at the top of your planting list!

Chard is actually a bottomless beet. It's in the same family as beets, but chard doesn't develop roots like beets. In the large, fleshy stalks and broad, crisp leaves, there are plenty of minerals and vitamins, just like the highly nutritious beet tops.

Plant chard in rows about 15 inches wide, scattering the seeds an inch or so apart. After thinning, the plants will be 4 to 5 inches apart. Harvest the first plants when they are about 6 inches high, and cut the entire plant an inch above the ground. In a short time the chard leaves come on again. Harvest only a few feet of the row at a time, so by the time you cut your way to the taller plants at the end of the row, the plants you harvested first are about ready to cut back again. This way the wide row of chard will keep producing all the way into fall and early winter.

If you really enjoy chard, make two plantings: one in early spring and another one in mid or late summer. You can plant it in the fall down South.

Chard comes in different colors. **Swiss chard** is green with white stems, and **rhubarb (or ruby) chard** has bright red stems and reddish-green leaves. I prefer ruby chard, partly because I like the

color it adds to the greens. Ruby chard also has more of a beety taste to me, and when the stalks get ahead of me and grow large, they are more tender than large Swiss chard stalks.

Those chard stalks, by the way, are a bonus vegetable for the greens grower. You can cut the stalk and thick mid-rib out of the leaves and have two entirely different vegetables from the same plant. Just cook up the leaves using your favorite greens recipes and prepare the stems as you would asparagus or braised celery.

GETTING READY
Planning on paper

When you think about greens to plant — you've got a big group of plants to consider, as well as different varieties of some salad crops. So plan your greens garden on paper when the temperature in the middle of the winter really drops down. It's a nice time to spend an evening or two thumbing through the summery, colorful seed catalogs.

In addition to my 'big three' of spinach, lettuce and chard, I make room for cabbage family greens, and some lesser known greens, such as chicory, corn salad, rocket and escarole. They don't take up much room, and a new green can really spice up a summer salad.

We plan to put our rows of lettuce, spinach, endive and other salad greens close to the kitchen door. Because we have salad so often and like it very fresh, we like to have the greens on the near side of the garden, so it's easy to gather what we need for a salad.

If you're going to plant your lettuce in space-saving wide rows for the first time, you'll have room to try several varieties. Buy an extra seed packet or two of varieties you'd like to try. Planting just 3 to 6-foot rows of 3 or 4 kinds of lettuce will give almost any family more than enough lettuce to eat.

If you live in the South, you may want to design your garden to give lettuce and spinach some shade, so they'll last a little longer when the warm temperatures come and push these crops toward bolting.

Planning Tips

Plan in advance to use methods of shading cool-weather greens, or try these planting ideas:

Plant lettuce under pole bean teepees to provide some shade. The bean foliage will shade some of the sun and keep the plants and soil cool. Plant the beans early.

Plant some lettuce or spinach between your corn rows, or on the shady side of a row of tomatoes.

Try multi-planting. Plant lettuce, carrots and

onions within the same wide row (15 or 16 inches across). Harvest the lettuce when young, leaving expansion room for carrots and onions. You can mix and match with other crops, too, including beets and spinach.

Save a window box for a hot green like curli-cress. Or, plant lettuce in a small section of your flower garden, or use it as a decorative, edible border. The foliage is lovely and contrasts beautifully with flowers.

Rich Soil: Greens Love It!

The healthiest and best-tasting greens are those that grow quickly. The important contributors to rapid growth are a steady moisture supply and a fertile soil, one rich with decomposed organic matter or humus.

Make it a point to regularly work plenty of organic matter into the top 6 to 8 inches of soil. Use leaves, compost, grass clippings, garden residues or easy-to-grow cover crops (buckwheat, cowpeas, annual rye grass).

Organic matter in the soil helps it to act like a sponge, retaining moisture. Without organic matter, the soil may drain too quickly, and shallow-rooted crops, like lettuce, will dry out and stop growing. When growth is interrupted like that, food quality goes way down.

When you spade or till all this organic matter into the soil, you are feeding the teeming soil life — those millions of micro-organisms that break down the organic matter into nutrient-rich humus. Feed them, and they'll feed you in return.

The micro-organisms in the soil and the plants' roots have to breathe, too, and organic matter gives the soil a porous quality so that oxygen can reach the roots.

If you have a heavy soil that doesn't drain well and crusts over after a rain, the particles of organic matter will wedge themselves between the tight, locked soil particles, so that air and water can circulate better.

I plant most of my greens in the spring — but the previous fall I add as much organic matter to my garden soil as possible. In mid-summer when I plant my fall crop of greens, I till in a spent spring crop such as peas or spinach — along with grass clippings or old mulch I have on hand — add some fertilizer and plant!

I'm wary of adding manures to the soil unless they're dehydrated or well-composted. Straight from the barnyard, manures contain many weed seeds that can germinate in your garden. Who needs extra weeds? The heat process of dehydrating or thorough composting kills most of the weed seeds. I know the dehydrated manures (available in 25, 40 or 50-pound bags in garden shops and supermarkets) are just about free of weed seeds.

To make your soil lighter you can also add sawdust to it, but don't overdo it. Mix only a layer of an inch or so into the soil in any one year, and add some nitrogen fertilizer along with it. Sawdust takes a long time to break down. Nitrogen is necessary for the soil organisms to do the job of decomposing, but that nitrogen is also needed by your plants for healthy, green leaves.

About pH

Lettuce, spinach, chard, beet and turnip greens, and most of the other greens, prefer slightly acid soil — soil with a pH of 6.0 to 6.5. pH is the measure of soil acidity or alkalinity. The pH scale of measurement runs from 1 (very acid) to 14 (very alkaline), with 7 as neutral. (In nature you would find the range between 4.0 to 8.3.) If your soil pH is too high or too low, your crops may disappoint you. Spinach, for example, will be stunted and less tender when the soil pH is down below 6.0.

To test your soil pH, you can buy an inexpensive testing kit at a garden store or send a soil sample to a commercial lab or to your local Cooperative Extension Service, if they do soil tests. The results may indicate you need to add pulverized limestone to raise your pH, or you may have to mix sulfur to the soil to lower your pH. Adding sulfur is not common in the East, but adding limestone is. Sulfur is sometimes necessary in the West.

The soil test report will indicate what and how much to add to your soil to bring it into the correct range.

A Scratch in Time Saves

When it's early in the season and nearly time to plant a host of greens, put in a little time with your garden soil to prevent weed problems.

For a week to 10 days before planting time, spade or till the soil every 2 to 3 days. This puts the soil in good tilth — no clods or soil chunks — and kills early-growing weeds. You see, weed seeds are quite small and must be near the surface where there is moisture and warmth before they can sprout to life.

When they do sprout, you have to look hard to see them. Working the soil — even raking it — will get rid of the tiny weed seedlings before they shoot up.

By periodically going over the soil before planting, you destroy most of the weeds that could be a problem later on. Work the soil one last time just a few minutes before planting. This eliminates most weed seeds that have germinated since your last outing and will give your greens an even chance against the few remaining ones.

Fertilizer

Most gardeners understand that vegetable crops need fertilizer to produce well, but sometimes the questions of what kind, when and how much can cause some confusion.

The nutrients your leafy greens need are available in commercial fertilizers such as 5-10-10 or 10-10-10, and in organic fertilizers like bonemeal, bloodmeal and dehydrated manures. By the way, the numbers 5-10-10 or 10-10-10 refer to the percentages of nitrogen (N), phosphorus (P) and potassium (K) in the bag of fertilizer. They're always listed in that order, too: N-P-K.

Nitrogen is essential to all growing vegetation for healthy, dark green leaves. Phosphorus helps plants grow strong roots and potassium or potash conditions the whole plant, helping it to bear fruit and resist disease. A balanced diet is important for plants, but remember that we're really looking for quick, steady leaf growth. Nitrogen is the key here. It gives our salad crops their dark green color and encourages stems and leaves to grow.

Of course, plants need more than just the three major plant nutrients to grow normally. There are secondary plant nutrients, such as magnesium, and some minor elements such as zinc and iron — all important, but usually plants need only small quantities. Most soils have most of these elements, but mixing good compost or a lot of organic matter like leaves or mulch into the soil insures the presence of these minor elements.

The best time to apply fertilizer is on the day you plant, because you want greens to grow fast.

To apply fertilizer, use this standard recommended amount: a 10 to 12-quart pail of balanced fertilizer, such as 5-10-10, for each 1,000 square

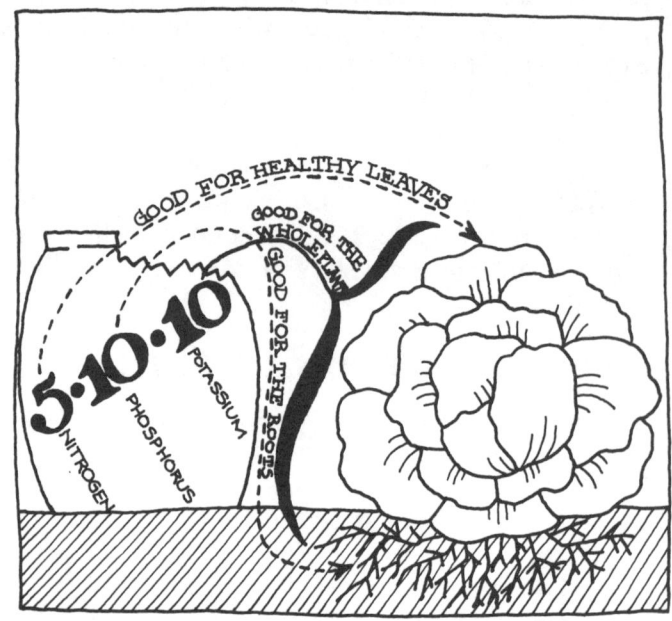

feet. For smaller plots, that comes to a couple of quarts for each 100 square feet. Simply toss it over an area as evenly as possible. You don't want to get a lot of the commercial fertilizer or dried manure in one place. Always mix the fertilizer into the top 2 to 3 inches of soil before planting. Seeds are sensitive and can get burned by any fertilizer that touches them, so spreading it evenly and mixing it into the soil prevents any trouble.

PLANTING
Wide Rows — Greener Garden

I've told you I plant my big three in rows 12 to 15 inches wide. Here's why:

Years ago, I planted my seeds like everybody else, in single rows — one seed behind another in a straight line. But after the plants were up, I got discouraged looking at the number of walkways in the garden and all the rich soil that would produce nothing but footprints.

So I started to experiment with wide row growing. Briefly, it involves broadcasting seeds in a wide band, thus creating thicker rows with fewer paths in between.

Not all vegetables, of course, are meant for wide rows. Squashes, tomatoes, cucumbers and melons are examples of crops that need room to run.

But for greens — including head lettuce, collards and kale — wide rows offer many advantages. Most importantly, we harvest over half again as much from wide rows as from single rows using the same space. With wide rows, it is finally possible to grow lots of spinach in a little space — plenty to eat fresh, plus enough to put by.

Many seasons of wide row growing and experimenting have shown more benefits than simply greater yields:

Wide rows mean less weeding because after the closely-planted greens grow up to shade the ground, they create a "living mulch" or ground cover that blocks out light from weeds, thus checking their growth. Some hand weeding is still necessary, but living-mulch wide-rows take care of most weeding.

Living mulch shades the soil, keeping it cool and moist, which is very important for crops like lettuce and spinach that get bitter and bolt when the weather warms up. Wide-row growing extends the harvest into summer because the soil in the row stays cooler. The cooler the soil — the better-flavored crop you'll enjoy.

With summer greens like Swiss chard, the moist soil of a wide row helps maintain continuous growth. There's less drying out of the soil, and consequently, less stop-and-go growth.

Planting is simple. You scatter seed over the wide seedbed with no worry about straight lines or precise spacing. Broadcasting seed is quick. I'm convinced you get a better stand of plants, too.

Wide rows are proven space-savers. You can do away with long single rows of one variety and plant more varieties of your favorite crops. For example, in a 10-foot-long row, 15 inches wide, you can grow 3 or 4 kinds of lettuce.

Harvesting is fast because you can reach so many more plants from one spot without moving. It sure beats the non-stop stooping and straightening it takes to harvest or weed single rows.

The garden looks nice. I couldn't believe the change in appearance of my garden when I started using wide rows. Try some wide rows — and give your garden a clean, lush look that will surprise you and your neighbors.

Time to Plant — Wide Rows

After you've prepared and fertilized your soil on planting day, follow these easy steps to plant your wide rows of greens and salad crops:

Mark the wide row. Stretch a string between two stakes close to the ground for the length of row you want.

Smooth the planting bed. With an iron garden rake, smooth the soil along one side of the string.

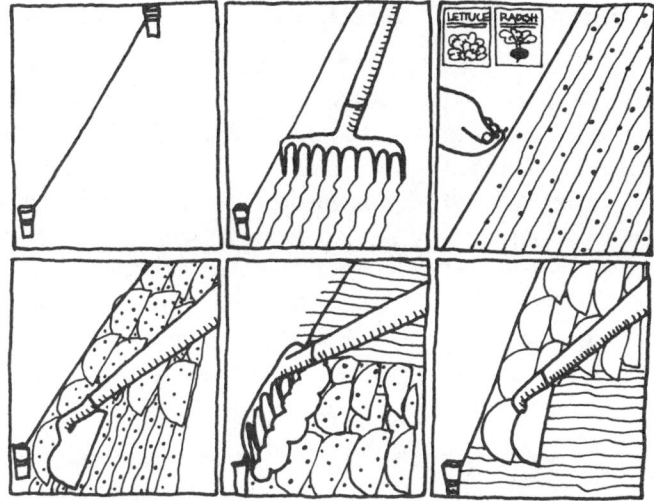

The rake will mark the width of the row. Don't pack the seedbed down by stepping on it. Always do your work from the side of the row.

Sprinkle the seeds onto the seedbed. Roll seeds off the ends of your fingers with your thumb. Try to scatter them across the seedbed as evenly as you can. The spacing of crops will vary a bit. Lettuce seeds can be planted much thicker than kale or collard seeds, for example. Don't worry if you plant too thickly, thinning will correct that. To give you an idea of how much seed you need, the average packet of lettuce seed will cover about 3 to 6 feet of a row 15 inches wide.

Sprinkle in a few radish seeds. After you've broadcast the main crop, sprinkle some radish seed down the row. They'll come up quickly and mark the row. I use about 5 percent as much radish seed as the main seed.

I have a hunch that radishes are decoys for some garden insects. Hungry pests seem to zero in on the first crop that appears in a row — radishes — and leave the others alone. After the regular crop is established, you can harvest the radishes.

Firm the seeds into the soil with a hoe, so the seeds make good contact with the earth.

Cover the seeds with soil from the sides of the row, pulling it up with your rake. The rule of thumb for the amount of soil to cover seeds is four times the diameter of the seed. So for most seeds in the green group, that's about 1/4 to 1/2-inch of soil. In mid-summer or late-summer plantings, an extra 1/4-inch of soil will help keep the seeds from drying out.

Finally, firm the soil once more with the back of a hoe and water gently if the soil is dry.

Single Row Planting

Use a string to plant a single row, too. Rake the seedbed smooth right over the string and with the handle end of your rake, make a shallow furrow or planting line along the string.

Sprinkle the seeds in the shallow furrow, and walk by a second time and drop radish seeds every 5 or 6 inches. After firming the seeds into the soil, cover them with 1/4 to 1/2-inch of soil and firm down gently again. Mark the row with the seed packet or a small sign, remove stakes and string and proceed to the next row to be planted.

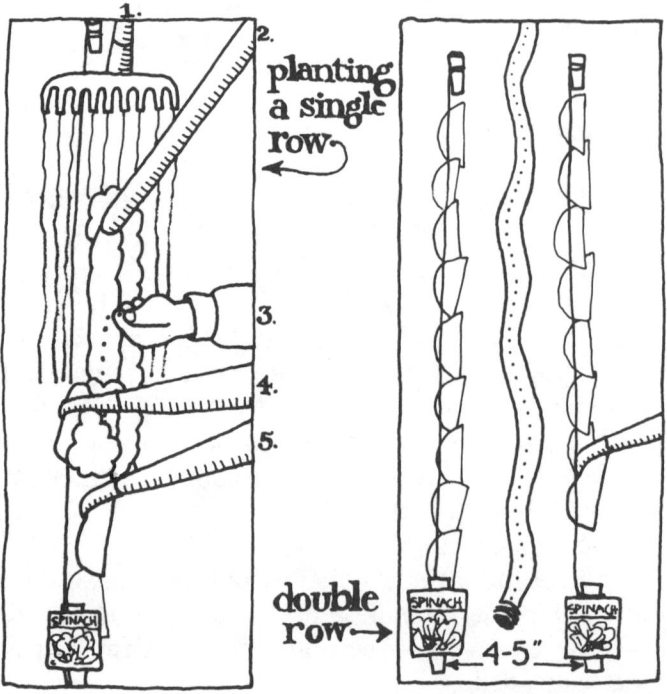

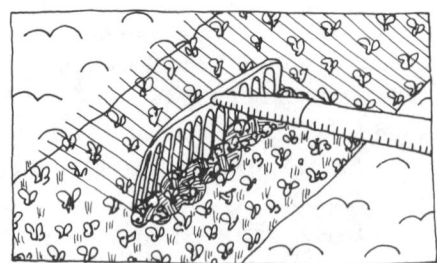

Double or Triple Rows

The double row planting system is just two single rows separated by 4 to 5 inches. It's a garden space-saver, and it is easier to irrigate, which is very important for gardeners in the West and South.

One irrigation system I've seen is simply placing a soaker hose between the two rows. A soaker hose has many tiny holes in it so water oozes gradually from it, irrigating only the soil around your plants. This is a big water-saving advantage over sprinklers which also water the walkways.

You can even put three or four single rows 4 to 5 inches from each other and move the soaker hose to each aisle to water all the plants. This arrangement has the space-saving characteristics of wide-row growing and lets you water all the plants evenly, too.

To Win — Thin!

To give your greens the best possible chance for success, thin! Whether you plant in wide, single, double or multiple rows, you'll need to thin. Because the seeds of most greens are so tiny, we all inevitably plant a little too thickly. That's not bad, though — it helps guarantee a good stand of plants.

You just have to thin out the crowd, so that the plants will have enough room to grow without too much competition from their neighbors. Thinning also provides good air circulation around plants to keep them from staying wet and becoming diseased.

Now, you can spend hours thinning by hand — or you can spend one minute using an iron rake. I pick the rake every time. To thin a row, simply pull the rake *across* it — with the teeth digging into the soil only about 1/4-inch. The teeth remove just enough seedlings, leaving the remaining ones properly spaced. Perhaps they look a little beat up, but don't panic. The plants will snap back quickly and get growing again, better than ever. Rake thinning also gets rid of many small weeds that may have started to germinate, again saving you tedious hand weeding time.

Thinning by hand has always seemed like too much work for me. But if you want the exercise, simply bend over and gently pull up enough plants, so the remaining ones are spaced correctly. For example, in the case of leaf lettuce, the plants should stand 3 to 4 inches apart, butterhead lettuce, 4 to 8 inches (6 to 10 inches if you want a bigger head). You can leave 6 to 10 inches between plants if you're thinning collards, kale or mustard.

THE WORLD OF GREENS

Two for the price of one

Beets and turnips are special greens because their roots are also edible. Beet greens are most nutritious and taste best when they're harvested young and tender. Fortunately, there's an easy way to have a lot of young greens and still keep plants in the garden for a long time to produce plenty of mature beet roots for later.

The secret is to plant beets in fairly thick wide rows. Beet seeds resemble tiny scraps of cork — they're bigger than most other salad and green crop seeds. They're easy to space correctly — about an inch apart.

Try about a 15-inch wide row if you haven't planted wide-row style before.

Plant early in the season. After the seedlings are up, thin with a rake and then sit back and wait for the green bonanza.

Start gathering your greens when the plants are about 6 inches tall. Pull up the entire plant, and if there's a small beet on the bottom, so much the better. Cook it right along with the greens for added flavor.

Detroit Dark Red and **Lutz** are the two good varieties. These produce excellent greens and good-sized, tasty beets, too.

A dish of turnip greens may sound like dreary eating — but only if you've never tried them. Cooked with salt pork or bacon, and served with butter or vinegar, greens can be a real taste treat — and very nutritious, too. Turnip greens are high in vitamins A and C, iron and calcium and are low in calories.

Turnips are a cool-weather crop, so plant them early in the spring — as soon as the ground can be worked — and again toward the end of summer for a fall crop. Spring is a great time to concentrate on their greens — you don't have to worry about summer heat spoiling any turnips underground. You simply harvest the plants when the roots are small before hot weather comes.

Fall plantings are popular in the South, too, because in most places you can plant anytime from August to October. The cool fall and mild winter temperatures keep the harvest going for several months. Of course, Southern turnip-lovers plant in the spring, too. In some Southern areas, you can plant every couple of weeks from February to May. With a system like that you'll have nothing but young, tasty greens.

Of course, I use wide rows when I plant turnips, usually about 15 to 16 inches across. In the South, where gardeners have boasted to me they were practically raised on turnip greens, I've seen 10 to 15-foot squares of greens in backyard gardens. Hardly anyone grows them in single rows because you get so few greens that way.

Plant turnips thickly, and once the plants are 4 to 5 inches tall, start thinning them by hand and boil up the tasty greens. You can eat a lot of greens this way and still afford to let some plants put on a good turnip root below ground.

Some people harvest just the big outside leaves from turnips, so the plants can produce more leaves from the center bud. I prefer to pull up the whole plant because the small leaves are the most tender.

You can have greens from any turnip variety, but a couple — **Seven Top** and **Shogoin** — are favorites because of their lush, tender foliage.

There's more information about growing and cooking beets and turnips in *The Gardens For All Book of Root Crops*.

Cabbage Family Greens
Mustard

Mustard — it's not yellow and you don't spread it on the backside of a ham sandwich. Garden mustard is leafy, curly, green and very nutritious. Down South I've seen mustard growing not only in vegetable gardens, but also in flower gardens as border plants.

Mustard planted in late summer for fall harvesting is tops. To me, cold weather and light frosts improve mustard's flavor, just as cold weather does good things for the taste of collards and kale. If you live where the winters are mild, plant mustard in late summer, and you'll harvest greens through the fall and into winter — mustard is quite hardy.

Of course, you can plant mustard early each spring, too. In as little as 30 days or so, you can be harvesting young leaves, or even the entire plant, if you grow mustard in wide rows. **Green Wave** and **Tendergreen** varieties give excellent results. Greenwave is peppery when raw, and Tendergreen has a nice mellow-green flavor when cooked.

Sow mustard seeds in rich, well-worked, fertilized soil. After the seedlings poke through the soil, thin them with a garden rake. After thinning, the plants should be 4 to 6 inches apart in the row. Start harvesting as soon as there is enough for a meal.

Collards — Headless Cabbages

The mild cabbagey taste and long tradition of collard greens at mealtime are really special for Southern gardeners. Collards are well-adapted to the climate in the South — unlike most greens, they'll survive not only the cool spring and fall weather, but also the intense heat of summer.

Some gardeners in the South plant a spring crop, harvesting the lower leaves as they need them early in the season. Then they simply keep the plants growing through the hottest months, and begin harvesting again in the fall. It's much more common, though, to plant collards twice, in early spring and again in late summer.

In the South, collards are so widely grown that garden stores and nurseries provide young collard plants for sale at planting time. Setting out these plants is a convenient and pretty reliable way to have a good harvest before hot weather slows things down.

The 4 to 5-inch seedlings resemble cabbage plants, but they'll never "head up" in the garden like cabbage. Some folks even refer to collards as "headless cabbages."

In the North you have to start collard seeds yourself. Most years I plant seeds directly in the garden for a fall crop, planting in mid or late July. I like the **Vates** variety of collards, but there are probably other good ones, too.

Fall collards profit from the cool nights and light freezes we have. That puts the zing and succulence into the leaves.

If you plant collards in wide rows, thin them, so that the plants will be 8 to 10 inches or so apart.

Like other greens, you can start harvesting collards as soon as some of the leaves make enough for a meal. If you harvest only the bottom leaves of the plant, the center bud (where the action is) will keep putting out branches.

Kale

Kale used to be more popular in our country. Before the days of trucking lettuce thousands of miles to market, local growers provided some of the big Eastern city markets with fall, winter and early spring kale. It helped fill the need for fresh, nutritious greens.

Kale is one of the very best greens if you're shopping for high vitamin and mineral content. It's sometimes called the "Wonder Crop" because its vitamin A and C content is so high. Kale even outranks orange juice in the vitamin C department.

Good taste goes hand in hand with its nutritional excellence. The leaves are tender and sweet-tasting when harvested at the right time, which is after a couple of hard frosts in the fall. The leaves develop a tanginess that is hard to match. Don't stop harvesting if the snows come. The plants stay green and tasty — all you have to do is dig through the snow to get them.

Another peak harvesting period for kale is when the snow melts in the spring and the plants start growing again. The leaves are delicious raw, or you can cook them and use them like spinach.

Kale is not a hard-to-grow or fussy plant. It simply needs well-fertilized, moist soil to get started. But like most cabbage family greens, after it comes up, you have to make sure it has enough moisture and thin the crop.

Kale doesn't like very hot weather — it's strictly a cool-season green. I like to plant the seeds in wide rows in July or August and start harvesting after our first fall frosts. In the South you can plant as late as October and have fresh kale through the mild winter into spring.

A few weeks after planting I thin the plants, so they are 6 to 8 inches apart. Later I can harvest entire plants to put a little more distance between the remaining plants and really give them room to grow.

Don't worry about mulching kale as winter approaches. I've found that while winter weather does kill some of the plants, most survive and put on good growth the following spring. The taste is very good until the plants bolt with warm weather.

Siberian Kale and **Blue Curled Scotch Kale** are the two varieties you'll most likely see in the seed racks. I think the Blue Curled Scotch variety is the better-tasting one.

By the way, the Blue Curled kale makes a nice houseplant in winter. Jan and I dig a couple up each fall, pot them and place them near a south-facing window. The plants lose some color, but the intricate shapes of the curled leaves are quite pleasing.

We also like to plant flowering varieties of kale. Their curly, green and maroon leaves are beautiful at the edge of the garden — and they also can be potted and brought indoors for the winter.

Cabbage Family Pests

Mustard, collards and kale are closely related to the cabbage — and so they suffer from similar pests and diseases.

If you plant any of these greens you'll have to watch for early season flea beetles, aphids and other insects. Spraying with Sevin or rotenone will control flea beetles — and malathion is recommended for aphids. Be sure to read all directions very carefully before you spray.

The best-known cabbage family pest is probably the cabbage worm — offspring of the white cabbage butterfly. As soon as you see the butterflies making the rounds of your garden, spray every 7 to 10 days with the biological control *bacillus thuringiensis*, available in garden stores as Dipel or Thuricide. It's a bacterium which causes the worms to get sick and die after they ingest it. It does not affect the crop or people who eat it.

To guard against diseases that plague the cabbage family of vegetables, be sure to rotate these crops each year. Do not plant them where any other member of the cabbage family — including cabbage, cauliflower, broccoli — grew the previous year.

Weeds & Cultivation

Weeds are green, too, but we really don't want them growing in among our salad crops. Some weeds are touted as highly nutritious when picked young — such as lamb's quarters and purslane. But I'm not a big fan of eating weeds, so I'll stick to vegetables that taste better, that have a longer harvesting season and that won't interfere with my other crops.

Most of the time weeds don't do us any good. They steal moisture, fertilizer and sunlight. Some of the slower-growing greens can be shaded out of your garden forever by weeds.

There are ways to avoid weed problems in any garden — even if you've suffered from weeding fits in the past:

Try to plant your fine-seeded greens in a section of garden that was relatively weed-free the season before. For example, where your thick, weed-smothering wide-rows of beans grew.

Work the soil with a shovel, rake or tiller every 2 or 3 days for a week or so before planting. This uproots the tiniest weed seedlings and kills them or buries them (which kills them, too).

Always work the soil just before planting. This clears away any newly-germinating weeds and at least puts any remaining weed seeds and your vegetable seeds on even footing.

Make your first thinning timely. When your vegetable seedlings are about 1/4 or 1/2-inch high, drag an iron rake across the row, keeping the teeth 1/4-inch deep. This thins the plants, of course, but it's also your first weeding effort.

Hand weed as often as necessary until the wide-row greens develop enough foliage to shade out further weed growth.

If you set out lettuce, collard or other transplants, work the soil before planting them, and wait a week or so for them to take hold before you cultivate near them.

In the first few weeks after being transplanted, the plants roots are quite close to the surface and gaining root strength by the day. Don't be careless

with a hoe and risk slowing them down or killing them. Keep all cultivation very shallow, 1/2 to 1 inch deep at most.

Use a good covering on the soil — a 'mulch' — to stop weeds around head lettuce plants, collards or plants in a single row. The hay, straw or other organic matter will stop most weeds except some stubborn perennials, which will grow through it. Pull those by hand.

Get after weeds when they are small. Don't even wait till they come up out of the ground. After a rain, which will surely cause some weed seeds to germinate, allow the soil to dry slightly and then lightly stir it up with your rake or weeding tool. You kill many weeds before they even appear.

Water

You can't beat greens that are crisp and succulent. One of the most important things for highest quality greens is a steady supply of moisture.

Greens thrive in moist, but not wet, soil. They require about an inch of rain or irrigation water per week, and perhaps a little more for summer greens in hot weather.

If the water supply drops, they may be the first crops in the garden to show signs of drought. That's because many of them — especially lettuce — have limited root systems; and because their large green leaves give off quite a lot of moisture. Sometimes on a hot, sunny afternoon many garden plants appear wilted. That's normal — usually they'll recover by next morning. If they don't, it's time to water.

Here are some tips to help you water wisely:

Irrigate early in the day to cut down on evaporation losses and to make your water go further. This also gives the plants plenty of time to dry out during the day. (Wet foliage overnight allows disease organisms to spread rapidly among plants.)

Soak the soil thoroughly enough, so that you don't have to come back and water again the following day. Try to moisten the soil to a depth of 5 or 6 inches at least.

If the soil is dry at planting time, water as gently as you can after planting, so you don't wash any seeds out. Be sure to keep the seedbed moist until the plants come up.

Diseases

I have not had too much of a problem with diseases affecting the greens and salad crops over the years. Occasionally, head lettuce develops a problem, perhaps bottom rot, which can occur during a streak of damp weather. These things happen, but don't be too concerned about them. As a home gardener, you can simply harvest heads no matter what size, cut out any damaged portion, and use them.

Another common ailment of head lettuce is tip-burn, where the ends of many leaves turn brown and die. It's mostly a hot-weather problem, and it's not caused by any pest or fungus in the soil.

Other diseases of head lettuce can be avoided by rotating the crop each year, not over-watering and spacing the plants in the row to ensure they have good ventilation.

Be sure to thin your wide rows of greens properly, so that the plants have enough air circulation to dry off after a rain or watering. If they're too thick, plants may stay wet too long and develop rot. Continual wetness is an invitation to disease.

Beet and chard greens sometimes develop leaf spot trouble. The edges of the greens turn dark brown and spots show up on the leaves, reducing the quality and appearance. However, it's not usually a serious problem. If the problem is bad, simply use a spray or dust containing Maneb, but read the directions carefully.

Also remember to rotate the cabbage family greens (kale, collards and mustard) each season to help avoid disease problems.

If you have any further questions regarding pests and diseases, check with your local County Cooperative Extension Agent. He or she will know about the problems in the area and will be able to suggest remedies.

Pests

Aside from the pests of the cabbage family greens, there are few pests that damage greens. Probably the most troublesome in most gardens are the small leaf miners, which feed on spinach, chard, beet and turnip greens. The larvae are 1/8-inch long, yellow and live in the leaves, while the adult fly is tiny, black and yellow. Spraying with malathion can control a bad problem. But at harvest time, just tear out the affected part and eat the rest.

Aphids and leafhoppers can also be a nuisance in some gardens. The six-spotted leafhopper spreads a virus among lettuce plants. They are light greenish-yellow, small but quite active. The United States Department of Agriculture recommends home gardeners spray with Sevin or malathion to control the leafhopper, beginning when the plants are 1/2-inch high and repeating once a week.

Many plants, including spinach and turnip, can be affected by the many kinds of aphids that suck sap from the leaves and spread diseases. Weekly spraying of malathion is recommended to control aphids. If you use malathion, pay attention to the directions carefully, and observe the recommended waiting times before harvesting.

Some of the more pungent greens like chicory, curlicress and celtuce seem to have fewer pest visitors.

Other pests I've noticed on or near my green crops have not really caused me a lot of headaches. Just plant enough of each crop to be able to sacrifice a small portion to insects and diseases.

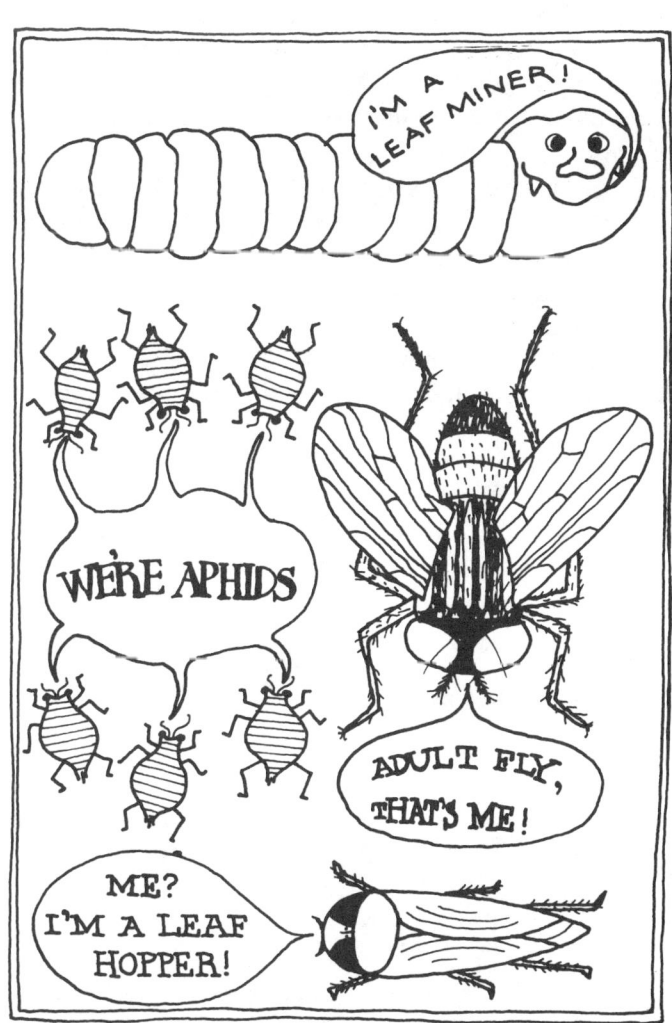

Curing Lettuce Problems

Let's look at some of the problems you may encounter growing all kinds of lettuce (and some other greens, too.)

"My seeds didn't come up." Don't write to the seed company right away. Most often, poor germination is caused by letting the seedbed dry out. It has to be continuously moist. Drying out occurs more often during hot weather plantings, and not as much with early spring plantings. Sometimes a light mulch of hay or straw to shade the soil after you plant will keep the soil moist until the plants are up. But don't delay in removing the mulch once you see the plants.

Also be sure to cover the seeds correctly — use just 1/4 to 1/2-inch of moist soil. If your soil gets very crusty and hard before the plants are up, gently run a lawn rake over the surface to break up the hard soil.

"My lettuce is bitter." Bitter lettuce is usually old lettuce, and the older it is, the worse it tastes. Harvest lettuce when it is young — as soon as there's something to eat — and harvest often. Don't wait for leaves to get big. Make frequent plantings of different varieties through the summer, so you'll always have tender sweet lettuce coming in.

"My plants go to seed before I harvest much." Seedstalks develop with warm weather and long days. It's the natural urge of a plant, and there's nothing you can do after lettuce bolts.

Bolting won't affect you if you make successive plantings and harvest early. Cut the entire plant off about an inch above the ground. Also, try slow-bolting varieties such as Oak Leaf which can take some heat.

Wide row planting slows bolting, too, as the close-growing plants keep the soil and roots cool.

Tips for Growing Head Lettuce

A lot of people think crisphead (iceberg-type) lettuce is hard to grow. It's not. Good head lettuce just needs fertile soil, ample sunlight, a good supply of moisture and nutrients — and most importantly, cool weather. The plants like temperatures around 55 or 60°F during the growing season, but sometimes it doesn't always work out that way.

Because head lettuce must grow the most in the spring before it gets hot, plant the seeds indoors in late winter — about 6 to 8 weeks before the average date of the last hard spring frost.

Plant the seeds in shallow seed boxes or 'flats.' Put the tiny seedlings in a sunny spot and keep them watered. About six weeks later, the plants are big enough to set in the garden. But before you do that, harden the plants off to get them ready for outdoor living. Place them in a protected spot outside for a few hours a day, lengthening the time they spend outside until they're out there all day.

Our *Gardens For All Book of Tomatoes* has a lot more information on starting seeds indoors, caring for seedlings and how to harden them off in case you need some extra advice.

Head lettuce can be started in cold frames if you live where the nights don't get too chilly in early spring.

Gardeners in mild winter areas or where the springs are long and cool, you can simply sow head lettuce seeds in the garden and thin the plants to stand 10 to 12 inches apart. In the deeper South, plant seeds out in the garden in the fall, and harvest the heads in late winter and early spring.

Some varieties are noted as "heat resistant" in the seed catalogs. These are worth trying if hot weather comes too quickly in your area.

I can remember years when my head lettuce was doing fine until an extended spring heat wave came along. High temperature over a period of time is nothing but trouble for head lettuce. The heads lose their firmness, the leaves get bitter, and diseases may erupt. So, keep cool — by using mulch, starting seeds indoors and planning a fall head lettuce crop.

Transplanting Head Lettuce

Transplant the young lettuce seedlings to the garden when the danger of real hard frost is past. They'll take a light freeze if they are hardened off properly.

I till the soil on planting day to get rid of any weeds that have germinated and to prepare a good, loose seedbed. I usually make a 20-inch wide row for my head lettuce.

Putting the plants 10 inches apart from each other is the best way to grow them. Some experts recommend 15 or even 18 inches, but I find advantages for closer planting.

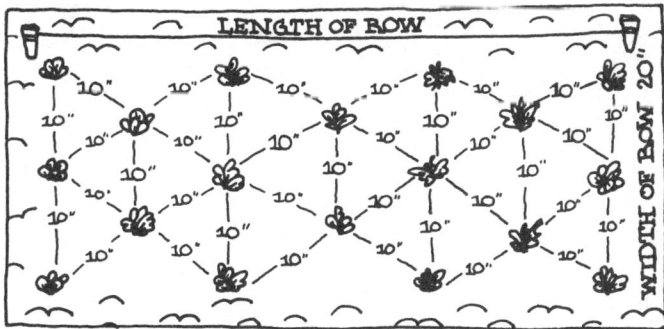

For one thing, you get more heads from a row, and they're better for eating than the larger ones that grow with wider spacing. I start harvesting heads when they're about the size of a softball — a most edible size. There's no waste and no storing.

You also have a continuous harvest if you start when the heads are small. If you wait until the first head you harvest is the size of a basketball, they'll *all* be that big on the same day. Start harvesting early, so that you'll have weeks of prime head lettuce. The quality drops off quickly once they reach maturity.

Another advantage to closer planting comes when the large outside leaves of the plants stretch out toward nearby heads. They form an effective shade cover for the soil. The soil stays cooler and more moist, which is necessary for good production. Weeds are also blocked out.

When setting the plants out, dig all the holes for them at one time, using a 10-inch scrap of wood to measure quickly the distance between holes. Dig each hole 4 to 5 inches deep. In the bottom of each hole put a tablespoon of 5-10-10 fertilizer or a small handful of compost or dried manure, and cover it with 2 to 3 inches of soil.

Water the flats well before transferring the seedlings to the garden. That will help keep soil around the roots and protect them from injury. Before you put them in the ground, strip the outer leaves off the plant. Don't touch the center sprout of the plant, though, because that bud will grow to form the head.

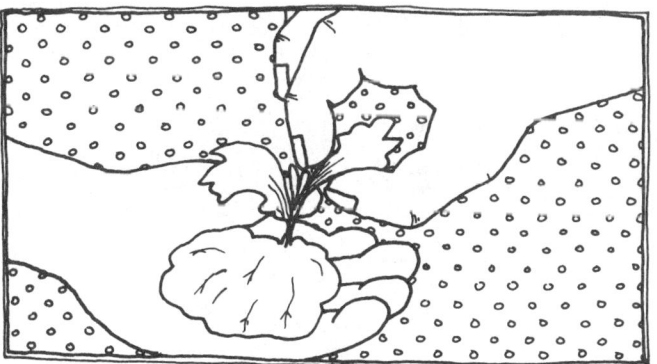

I trim the foliage because some of the roots are killed in transplanting, and the smaller root system can't support all the top growth. The roots, which need time to recover, take hold and start to grow again, and find it easier at first to meet the demands of fewer leaves.

Set the plants in slightly deeper than they were in the flats and give them a gentle watering. Keep them well-watered for a few days.

Mulching

A thick, organic mulch (straw, leaves, grass clippings, hay, etc.) is almost a must if you're

growing head lettuce down South in the spring. It will help retain moisture and keep the soil cool as warm spring weather arrives. It's good in Northern gardens, too, where spring heat or quick-draining soils could hurt the crop.

Cultivation

Cultivation is simply stirring up the soil lightly to kill young weeds and to aerate the soil. Be sure not to till or hoe around your head lettuce plants deeper than 1 inch — their roots are shallow.

Booster Shot

Head lettuce, like the other kinds of lettuce, has a limited root system and can't go deep in the soil for nutrients. Sometimes an application of extra fertilizer along the way — sidedressing — can help.

Some gardeners like to put down compost after harvesting to help spur new growth. My soil usually has enough nutrients present, so I don't have to do this. But if you have the compost and time to do it — go ahead. You can sidedress with 10-10-10 or bonemeal, too.

To sum up — good head lettuce needs fertile soil, ample sunlight, a good supply of moisture and nutrients — and most importantly, some cool weather. The plants like temperatures around 55 or 60°F during the growing season, but sometimes it doesn't always work out that way.

Lettuce Tip for Roadside Stands

You can grow such a great amount of leaf lettuce in a small space that it can be a rewarding cash crop for a little roadside stand — if you can offer it fresh to the customer. Leaf lettuce is rarely in the supermarkets because it doesn't stay fresh for very long.

To keep it crisp at your stand, put it in a cooler with some ice on the bottom. Moisten a towel or cloth and spread it over the lettuce to keep moisture in. Set the cooler in the shade and put a sign on it to let people know there's tasty, fresh leaf lettuce inside.

Heading into Fall

Not enough people realize it is easy to have nice fall heads of lettuce, too. Gardening in Vermont, I start the seeds in flats in partial shade by the side of the barn. Sometimes I start the seeds directly in the garden toward the end of July.

Most years it requires a watchful eye during the first few weeks of growth to make sure the plants don't get parched and burned by the sun. They must have a good supply of moisture.

If you start seeds indoors, wait until they're 3 to 4 inches high before transplanting them. The best time to put them out is after a few rainy days or during some cool weather.

And Still More Greens

Endive

Endive is a cool-weather green with a distinct, clean, sharp taste. In recent years it has shown up more often in the produce bins of stores but it's still expensive.

Endive doesn't like hot weather too well, but it can take some pretty hard frosts. So it's a good green down South where the winters are mild. Up North we grow it as a spring or fall crop only. I'm usually too busy with other crops in the spring, so I plant endive in late July or so for a fall picking. It's a good green to follow my first crop of snap beans.

Plant the seeds directly in the garden, keeping the soil moist until they come up. Plant them in wide rows and thin later with 6 to 7 inches between plants. You can start endive in flats indoors like head lettuce and transplant them later if you want.

Like other greens, endive tastes best when it grows quickly and steadily. Make sure it gets enough water and fertilizer.

To reduce the bitterness of endive cut off the light to the heads, or "blanch" them, right out in the garden about a week before harvesting them. Gather up the leaves of the plant and tie them together above the head or cut the tops and bottoms out of milk cartons and slip these homemade blanching tubes over the plants.

I like the curly-leaf endive varieties such as **Green Curled.** The green known as 'escarole' is actually a less-curly endive with broader leaves, grown the same way as 'endive.'

Chicory

Chicory grows wild in many parts of the country. It's easy to recognize in fields or along the road when the plants sport many small blue flowers in late

summer. But by the time wild chicory flowers, the greens are practically inedible. If you locate the wild plants early in the spring, try harvesting some of the spiny young leaves for salads.

Two different cultivated harvests are possible from a row of chicory: you can pick young leaves early in the season or let the plants grow (but not allowing seedstalk to develop) and harvest the roots after a killing frost in the fall. The roots can be roasted and ground and used as a substitute for coffee — a practice that started 200 years ago in Italy when coffee became a fashionable but expensive drink. Or, the roots can be placed in a cool cellar and the tops "forced" for fresh salad sprouts in winter. The greens in this case are often called **witloof** heads. That's from the Dutch word for "white leaf." In Europe, forcing witloof heads is big business. For an American home gardener, it can be a rewarding winter project.

Chicory should be planted in late spring or early summer. Sow the seeds in a wide bed, a foot or so across. If you have loose, rich soil somewhere, great! That will encourage the plants to develop large, straight roots. After the plants come up, thin them to 4 or 5 inches apart. You can harvest the greens for salads, or you can let the plants grow if you're interested in the roots.

Winter Chicory or French Endive

Chicory roots can be forced in the fall or in the dead of winter to have nice tight heads of fresh leaves for salads. Forcing simply means encouraging the roots to use their stored energy to send up fresh top growth.

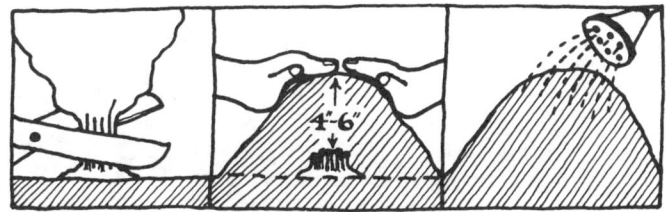

You can do this right out in the garden in early fall if you want. Just cut the top of the plants off about one inch above the crowns, hill 4 to 6 inches of soil over the plants and keep the roots watered.

I think it's better to harvest the roots, store them and force them in the cellar in midwinter when a fresh head of chicory is really a delight.

Dig the roots sometime after the first killing frost. Don't brush them or wash them. Just place them in the sun for an hour or so. Then store them in a cool cellar (40°-50°F) in sand, sawdust, peatmoss or in plastic bags.

When winter sets in, take some chicory roots and trim the root ends so they're pretty much the same length — probably around 6 to 8 inches.

Get a box that's twice the height of the roots and half fill it with sawdust, sand, peatmoss or very fine soil. Put the roots in standing upright, close together but not touching each other. The crowns of the roots should just be at the top of the packing material. Water thoroughly and then top off the box with another 6 inches or so of more fine sand, peat or sawdust. Put the box out of the light in a warmer spot (60° is recommended as ideal) and keep the earth moist. Cover the box with plastic or newspaper to keep the moisture in. In 3 or 4 weeks you can harvest the tightly folded leaves that sprout up from the center bud of the crown.

You may have to water again if the lower packing material dries out a bit. Make a hole through the top layer to water. You don't want it wet where the leaves are growing.

The heads are usually just an inch or two in diameter and 5 or 6 inches tall. The leaves are yellowish or white because they haven't received any light. Separate the leaves before serving them.

You can start forcing a box of roots every 2 weeks or so to have a supply throughout the cold months.

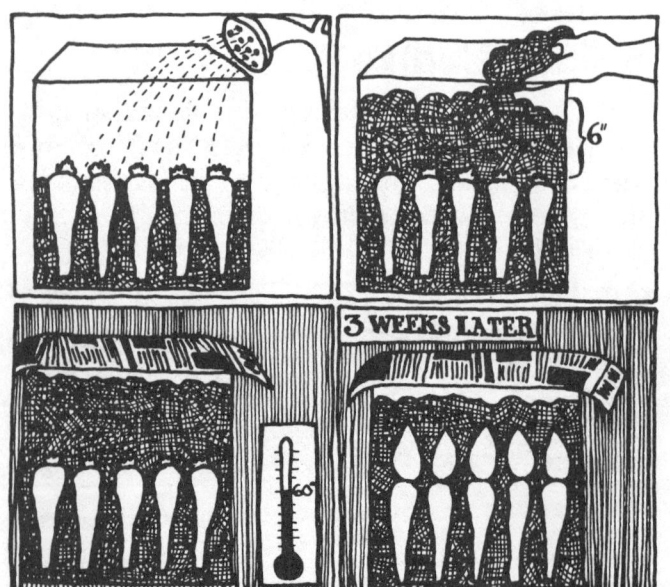

Rocket

Rocket is sometimes called "ruccola" or "rocquette" in seed catalogs. It's one of a number of salad greens I've started to grow in recent years in a special fall section of the garden.

The young leaves are rough and slender, with a taste all their own — hot, with a hint of bean or nut flavor. Chopped into a salad, the leaves can sure keep people guessing about the ingredients.

Dandelion

I've never really met a dandelion I liked. I'm as surprised as most people to see the seeds for sale in garden stores. I've tried eating the young, spiny leaves of dandelions growing wild, but frankly, I've never found them that appetizing. But other people really like them.

Dandelion greens are more popular in Europe, I'm told. It's there that several dandelion varieties

were developed to produce larger and curlier leaves. European gardeners make a habit of blanching the plants to reduce bitterness.

If you want to blanch some local dandelions — maybe on your lawn — turn flower pots over them early in the spring, wait a week and then harvest the leaves.

It's just hard for me to think about planting dandelions as they can be hard to root out if they get firmly established in the garden. If you're a determined gardening experimenter and want to grow some, plant the seeds in spring as soon as you can work the soil. Thin them to 3 inches apart and later to about 5 or 6 inches. Keep picking the green leaves as they reach edible size and as long as you can eat them.

I've heard that you can dig up the dandelion roots — wild or garden varieties — and force them in the cellar like rhubarb or chicory roots, but until I try it, I won't recommend it.

Corn Salad

I didn't know very much about this spring and fall green before I planted it. Some U.S. seed companies introduced this European specialty a few years ago and I decided to try it. (It's sometimes called lamb's lettuce, fetticus or maches.)

One of the nice things about corn salad is its hardiness. It's one of the last crops to quit in the fall and early winter. You get plenty of light green leaves for salads. They don't have much taste, so you should mix them with other salad greens.

I sow the seeds fairly thickly toward the end of our hot summer weather. I usually plant a row 10 feet or so long and 15 inches wide, simply by broadcasting the seed over the seedbed. After thinning, the plants will be a few inches from each other. You can plant it in the spring, too, if you like, but I save it for the fall, since it takes cold weather so well.

Like other greens I like to harvest as soon as there's something to eat — after just 3 to 4 weeks — by cutting the whole plant right above the ground. They are never too tall, but the leaves are fairly wide, so it's easy to fill a salad bowl.

Though our long, wide row probably yields more corn salad than necessary, it's nice to know that we have fresh greens still growing as the early winter snow clouds head our way.

Celtuce

Celtuce was introduced to U.S. gardeners more than 20 years ago from China, but it didn't meet with much success. I've seen more seed catalogues carrying it now, so perhaps it's getting another try from gardeners.

It was first called "celery lettuce." That's be-cause you can harvest the young leaves of the plants in early spring like leaf lettuce, and then later as the plants get taller, cut the stems, pick off the leaves, peel them and use them like celery, raw or cooked.

Celtuce is a cool-weather plant for the most part. You should plant it as early as you plant lettuce, but spaced a little farther apart. Harvest the leaves as they reach eating size.

The late spring warm weather will cause the leaves to become bitter, so let them go. When the plant gets a foot or two high, cut the stalk for the "celery" harvest. Trim the leaves off and be sure to peel the stem before eating raw or cooking.

Curlicress or Peppergrass

I like the name curlicress for this zesty, fast-growing green because the plants are low to the ground, frizzy and add a curly look to the salad garden.

It's often advertised as the plant you can start harvesting in 7 to 10 days. I've come pretty close to that in my garden.

Curlicress will grow just about anywhere. Probably the best place for it would be in an indoor flat near the kitchen where you could snip leaves anytime for garnishing salads or sandwiches.

Chew a few leaves before you decide to use a lot of it in any one dish, though. Curlicress has a firey taste.

Plant it in short, thick rows early in the year and throw more seeds in every couple of weeks. Harvest early because it will produce little flower stalks in a month or so and the quality of the sprigs will go down.

Watercress

Most people think they have to chase around the woods and streams to find watercress. Not so. Though it is more at home in a fast, shallow stream, this snappy, clean-tasting green will grow very well in the garden. You just have to give it a wet spot — preferably some shade, too — to grow in. You'll have to water it often to assure rapid growth.

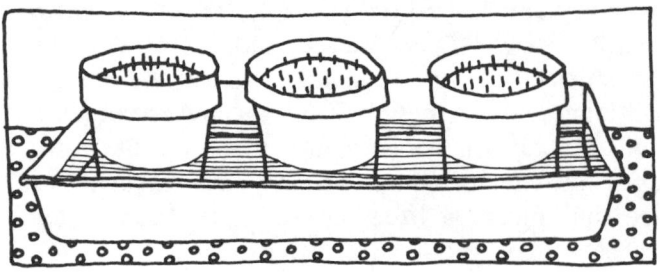

You can start seeds in small, clay pots set in a pan of water indoors and later transplant them to an outside location when the hard spring frosts are past. Or you can start some plants indoors by sticking some store-bought leafy watercress stems in moist potting soil. Just make sure you keep it well watered.

When the stems start producing new leaves, you can transplant them to the garden about 6 to 8 inches apart from each other. In 4 to 5 weeks, you can start harvesting by cutting off the top 3 to 4 inches of the plants.

Giving the plant the moist conditions it needs will be any gardener's main challenge with watercress. Once you find the right spot . . . perhaps next to a small pool, or in a low, wet area of the garden . . . then you can show off your success with this somewhat rare and highly-prized green. It really adds flavor to sandwiches, omelettes, fresh-caught trout and jazzes up salads.

Watercress Stream

A friend showed me how to create a false stream on the shady side of the house to grow watercress. Dig a trench (preferably near a downspout or an outside spigot) that will hold a few sections of orangeburg pipe, cut in half lengthwise. (Orangeburg pipe is a man-made fiber pipe — often 6 inches in diameter — used in sewage systems.) You can cut it with a saw. Incidentally, because you're cutting it in half, just buy half the total length you want to end up with.

Butt the sections together and place them in the trench, so the rim of the pipe is at ground level. Just about fill the pipe with small stones or stone chips. Then place narrow, perforated plastic seed flats in the pipe trench. Fill them with peat moss and soil, and sow your watercress seeds or put in cuttings.

Let the water from a garden hose or the spigot run into the stones in the pipe sections. As long as the stone bed beneath the flats stays wet, your watercress should flourish — from first thaw to last freeze.

If you have a drainage problem where you've built your stream, you can run a "lateral" of perforated soil drain from one of the ends.

Upland Cress

I haven't grown upland cress yet, though I have a jar of seeds that a gardening friend saved for me that I'm looking forward to planting. This cress, sometimes called winter cress or spring cress, is a biennial, which means that it will go to seed the second year of its growth.

You plant seeds early in the spring, and soon after start harvesting the young leaves and sprigs. The plants will survive most winters and send up flower stalks early the next season. You can have a spring harvest of some leaves before the seedstalks appear.

The seeds of upland cress must be easy to harvest because my friend sent me a whole handful of them.

Celery

Celery has a reputation for being a fussy, hard-to-grow vegetable. There's a lot of truth to that, but with the right climate and some care, you can grow large, tender celery. A dozen plants will take up just 5 or 6 feet of row, and it's worth trying.

Celery is challenging to grow because it needs a long time to grow — up to 130 to 140 days of mostly cool weather — and it's quite demanding when it comes to water and fertilizer. If your soil stays moist and has plenty of organic matter in it, you're in good shape for growing celery. But shut off the water supply even for a short time, and you're in trouble.

The roots of celery plants are limited — usually stretching just 6 to 8 inches away from the plant and only 2 to 3 inches deep, so the top part of the soil not only has to have enough moisture, it must also contain all the nutrients the plants need.

Celery plants don't like hot weather at all — the crop will thrive only where the winters are mild, or where the summers are relatively cool, or where there's a long, cool growing period in the fall. In Vermont the summers are not blisteringly hot, so we can set out plants in the spring, tend them through the summer and harvest a crop in early fall.

Because celery takes such a long time to grow, it's best to start the seeds in plant boxes or flats indoors to get the jump on the season.

Celery seeds are slow to germinate, so soak them overnight to speed up the process. Plant them indoors around 12 weeks before the last frost.

When the plants are 2 inches high, transplant them to individual peat pots or to another deeper flat with new potting soil. If you use flats, put the plants at least 2 inches apart.

By early May the plants are about 4 to 6 inches high. Harden them off for a week to 10 days to get them used to the spring weather.

Transplant celery a week to two before the average date of the last frost. However, experts say that if the weather turns cold after you set them out (night temperatures consistently under 55°F) the celery plants may go to seed prematurely. Well, we have our share of cool spells in Vermont, and I can remember only two or three plants going to seed early. Because of the need for a long season, it's worth the gamble to set them out early — they'll

take any light frost we have in May.

To transplant celery, first work the soil, mix in the fertilizer (about 1 pound of 5-10-10 per 30 square feet) and dig a straight trench about 4 to 5 inches deep. Plant the celery in the bottom of the trench, spacing the plants 8 to 10 inches apart, and set them half an inch deeper than they were in their pots.

Remove some of the outside leaves from each plant before setting them in. As with head lettuce, this trimming helps the roots recover from the transplant shock and resume normal growth more quickly.

As the plants grow, fill in the trench with sand or soil, mulch or compost. This blanches the lower part of the stalks, and also keeps the roots cool, which celery plants like.

I've also grown celery in 'blocks' instead of furrows. The blocks measured about 3 to 4 feet on each side. It's a real space saver.

Cultivation is important because celery grows slowly and doesn't appreciate any competition from weeds, and remember to keep your weeding shallow, so you don't injure the celery roots.

Sidedressings of 5-10-10 or similar balanced fertilizer in the second and third month of growth will help keep celery growing steadily. Use 1 tablespoon per plant and sprinkle it in a shallow furrow about 3 to 4 inches from the plant and cover it with soil.

Give your plants plenty of water. If celery is short on moisture, or a hot spell hits, the stalks get tough and stringy. They can also develop hollow or pithy stalks in dry spells.

When celery gets big enough to eat, start harvesting the larger, outer stalks as you need them. The center will keep producing stalks. To harvest big plants at the end of the season, simply pull up the whole plant and trim off the roots.

Blanching

Unblanched celery is twice as strong in flavor as the celery you buy in the store. I like celery a little milder in taste, so I take the time to blanch the stalks before harvest — simply keeping the sun from striking the stalks.

Open the tops and bottoms of half-gallon milk cartons and use these 'sleeves' to blanch your celery. Set the cartons over the plants a week, 10 days or even longer before you want to harvest. The color of the stalks will lighten, and their flavor will become milder.

Some people place boards close along each side of the row to blanch celery. Others simply bring soil or mulch up around the plant to block out the sun. If you use soil, wait until the cool weather of early fall arrives and hill up the plants when they are dry and free of disease. This will help prevent rot. There's no need to blanch the top leaves, of course, just the stalks.

Storing

Celery stores really well — you can keep it for many weeks with no trouble. Dig up the plants carefully, disturbing the roots as little as possible. Replant them in boxes of sand in your root cellar or set them close together in a trench in your cold frame where you can keep them from freezing. As long as the roots stay moist and the stalks dry, they'll really keep. Temperatures in the range of 35 to 40°F are best for good storage.

HARVESTING

Harvesting is one of the nicest chores of the gardening season. It's easy to do right:

Start harvesting when there's something to eat. Gardens are for eating, so as soon as your endive, spinach, celery, lettuce or whatever is big enough to toss in a salad — harvest. There will be plenty more to come.

Harvest at peak flavor and freshness. Young greens are the tastiest and most nutritious. Don't wait for prize-winning heads of lettuce — start picking them when they're soft-ball size — still crisp and flavorful.

If you're freezing or canning spinach, chard or beet greens, harvest the choicest leaves and plants and process them right away for the best quality.

Harvest lettuce and other greens close to meal time to retain as much quality and food value as possible.

Try for 2, 3 or even 4 cuttings. Leaf lettuce and chard are the best examples of crops that will "come again" after you harvest. If you cut lettuce and chard an inch above the ground, the plants will send out new, fresh growth in an effort to make seed. This is the way I harvest all lettuce varieties except crisphead. It seems drastic, but it's not.

With Oak Leaf lettuce I sometimes get 4 cuttings in a season. And the produce is much sweeter than what I'd get by just picking off the larger, more mature leaves that can be somewhat tough and bitter.

Incidentally, a long serrated bread knife is the best tool for harvesting wide rows of greens.

Easy Cold Frames

A cold frame can extend your green season no matter what part of the country you live in. Cold frames are basically little houses where greens can have a head start in spring and extra growing time in the fall and early winter.

Probably the simplest cold frame I ever built was just six bales of hay arranged in a rectangle on the southern side of the house and topped with a storm window. I just planted my greens seeds in a flat and placed it in the center of the bales underneath the glass.

If you have an old storm window and some planks or scrap lumber, you can put together another easy cold frame. Most designs I see call for slantwise cutting of lumber, hinges, permanent locations and more work than is necessary. There is a simpler way.

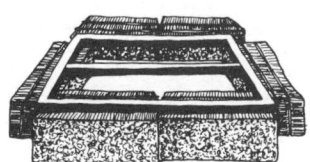
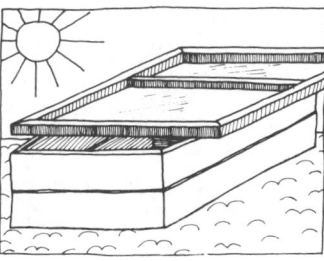

Nail the wood together to fit under the storm window you have. Instead of cutting wood on the slant, just build the frame as a box and simply top it with the storm window. Skip the hinges. On hot days, slide the window to the side to let heat out; on cold nights, put the window squarely over the top of the frame and cover it with an old blanket. In the summer when you don't need it, it's easy to store.

Cold frames are good for starting seedlings early in the season for later transplanting or for just growing some lettuce, spinach and radishes to eat early. In the fall you can grow Boston and other loosehead lettuce and some leaf lettuce for the last homegrown salads in your neighborhood.

Dear Friends —

Now that the greens are grown and harvested, it's my turn. I am happy to share what I have learned over the years about preparing and serving greens as well as keeping them for when they aren't available fresh from your garden.

It's difficult for me to pick my favorite vegetable or even group of vegetables, but greens rank high for both me and my family. Over the years we've invented dishes and salads we enjoy, and discarded others that weren't so great. Only the ones we really like are included here. I hope you like them, too.

Jan Raymond

Jan Raymond

FAVORITE RECIPES
Salads

Good salads are easy to make, and they are wonderful. Unfortunately, bad salads are also easy to make. The two most important rules for excellent salads, I think, are

1) use the freshest, cleanest greens available and

2) use no commercial dressings.

The first rule is challenging for me only in the deep of winter. At that time of year, I am hard-pressed to find nice greens. But many of you don't live as far north, and it's easier for you to have fresh, home-grown greens later in the year.

The second rule isn't challenging at all, because tasty salad dressing is so easy to make. Basic oil and vinegar dressing — vinaigrette — takes me less than two minutes from start to finish. If I want to dress it up a bit, it may take a minute longer. Of course, I can make it more complicated, but it's not necessary. If I really want to save energy, I can make up a whole jar of basic dressing and make additions for each salad right in the bowl — it keeps in the refrigerator for up to a month.

Good quality ingredients are important for the best flavor. Although I have used corn oil and other vegetable oils with success in vinaigrette dressing, I prefer the flavor of olive oil. A mild vinegar — perhaps a wine or herb vinegar — gives just enough tartness without overpowering the flavor of the entire dressing. No matter how much dressing I make, the proportion of oil to vinegar remains the same: 3 to 1.

Basic vinaigrette dressing

3   Tb olive oil
1   Tb vinegar
1/4 tsp dry mustard
     salt and freshly ground pepper

If I make up a jar of dressing, I may add a couple of peeled garlic cloves plus salt, pepper and dry mustard, and that's it until I am ready to make a salad. Dry mustard may not be used by purists, but I find it gives the dressing a little sparkle many people enjoy. (When I first started using dry mustard in dressing, I was a little heavy handed, and everyone could guess my new, secret ingredient — so, go easy!)

I mix the basic dressing in the salad bowl and then decide what seasonings and extras I want to add to complement the meal. It may be fresh herbs — a terrific one is dill, another standby is basil; it may be cheese — almost everyone likes some Roquefort or bleu crumbled in their dressing; perhaps some chopped green pepper or onion. I try to do this as I start preparing the meal, so they have sufficient time to "stew." Then just before bringing the bowl to the table, I'll put the lettuce on top of the dressing and add any garnish I want. Just before serving, the salad gets a good toss, so the greens are evenly and lightly coated with dressing.

One easy way to wreck a salad is to use too much dressing. It can drown the salad and make the lettuce limp and soggy. If you find that there's a lot of dressing in the bowl after the salad is gone, you're probably using too much dressing — hold back a little.

Greens preparation

In the summer I like to pick lettuce from the garden just minutes before serving. I wash it well and don't chill it because it's so fresh. Actually, I think that the flavor of lettuce is enhanced if it's close to room temperature rather than icy cold. Others, however, prefer lettuce cold, because it's crisper.

If I need to store lettuce, I wash it first, wrap it in a damp towel and store it in a plastic bag or tightly covered container in the refrigerator.

Washing lettuce is very important, because greens are magnets for dirt. Nothing ruins a salad faster than having grit as the surprise ingredient.

Because oil and water don't mix, lettuce leaves also need to be dried before being mixed with salad dressing. If they are not dry, they won't accept a coating of oil, and the dressing will just end up in the bottom of the bowl.

Wash leafy greens in several changes of water, letting the grit settle to the bottom and lifting out the greens while changing the water. Be careful not to bruise the leaves.

To dry leaf lettuce, wrap the leaves lightly in a clean towel and pat dry. You can also drain them in a colander or swing them in a wire salad basket. Many people also swear by salad spinners for drying and storing lettuce.

To wash head lettuce, core the solid part of the stem and hold the head upside down under running water. Place on a terry towel in the refrigerator and cover with another towel. In a few hours the lettuce will be dry.

Unless you are cutting wedges of tightly-packed head lettuce, such as iceberg, it is suggested that you tear lettuce greens by hand rather than cut them with a knife. I believe there is a difference in flavor, and I like hand-torn lettuce best. I have tried to discover if there were any nutritional reason for recommending tearing, and so far I can't discover any. For many, sufficient reason seems to be — "My mother told me to do it that way." What I recommend is try both and see which you prefer.

Basic blender mayonnaise

Although Vinaigrette dressing is my stand-by, I do use some others. The most basic, of course, is mayonnaise. It's not hard to make because I use a blender. Homemade mayonnaise really does taste quite different and much better than store-bought. As for economy, I think I save about a nickel a gallon, but as I make it in small batches, I probably don't save anything.

1	egg
1/2	tsp dry mustard
1/2	tsp salt
	dash of cayenne pepper
2	Tb lemon juice
1	cup salad oil, olive oil or mixture

Put egg, mustard, salt and cayenne in blender and blend for 30 seconds at high speed. Add lemon juice and blend for additional 10 seconds. While blending at high speed, very gradually add oil — in droplets, especially at first. Use rubber spatula if necessary to keep ingredients flowing to processing blades.

All of a sudden in the process, the sound will change as the mayonnaise thickens, and then you know it's almost done. Go very gently at this point in adding additional oil. Mayonnaise is an emulsion or suspension of egg in oil, and the oil can only hold so much before the whole thing separates. If it does separate, don't despair. Simply remove the mixture from the blender and start with another egg. After it is beaten thoroughly, gradually add the mixture to it and perhaps just a little more oil until it has reached the right consistency.

For different tastes, add one or a combination of the following to the mayonnaise base:

Almonds, chopped	Dry sherry	Parsley
Anchovies	Egg,	Pickles
Basil	hard-cooked	Pimiento
Catsup	Fennel	Sour cream
Capers	Garlic, minced	Spinach leaves,
Chervil	Green pepper	chopped
Chili powder	Horseradish	Tabasco sauce
Chili sauce	Nasturtium	Tarragon
Chives	leaves	Tomato, chopped
Curry powder	Olives	Watercress
Dandelion greens	Onion, grated	Whipping cream
Dill	Paprika	Yogurt

Creamy salad dressing

1	tsp egg yolk
1/2	tsp dry mustard
1/2	tsp minced garlic
	dash of Tabasco sauce
	salt and freshly ground pepper
1	tsp vinegar
1/2	cup olive oil (or peanut, vegetable or corn oil)
1 to 2	tsp lemon juice (fresh, preferably)
1	tsp heavy cream

Beat an egg yolk and put one tsp of it in a mixing bowl. Add the mustard, Tabasco sauce, garlic, salt, pepper and vinegar. To blend the ingredients well, beat with a wire whisk. Gradually add the oil, beating vigorously until dressing is thickened and well blended. Add the lemon juice and beat in the heavy cream. Makes about 3/4 cup, sufficient for 10 to 12 cups of salad greens.

Hot Bacon Dressing

1/4	lb bacon
1/2	cup diced onion
1/4	cup white vinegar
1/4	cup red wine vinegar
1/4	tsp salt
	pinch of pepper
1/4	tsp sugar
1 1/2	tsp cornstarch
1/2	cup beef broth

Sauté bacon in large pan until crisp. Drain.
Sauté onion in bacon drippings until soft. Stir in vinegars, salt, pepper and sugar.
Blend cornstarch and 2 Tb of beef broth in a small cup. Add remaining broth to pan and stir in corn starch mixture.
Cook over low heat, stirring constantly until thick. Pour over salad greens and toss. Sprinkle with crumbled bacon and serve.

Creamy Thousand Island Dressing

1/2	cup mayonnaise
1/2	cup chili sauce
1	tsp Worcestershire sauce
2 or 3	drops Tabasco sauce
1/2	tsp salt
1/4	tsp paprika
2	Tb chopped celery
2	Tb pickle relish
2	Tb stuffed olives, chopped
1	tsp minced onion
1	hard-cooked egg, chopped
1/2	cup sour cream

Combine mayonnaise, chili sauce, Worcestershire, Tabasco, salt and paprika in a bowl. Mix in remaining ingredients except for sour cream. Fold in sour cream. Chill well. Will keep in the refrigerator for up to one month. Makes 1 pint.

Tangy Russian Dressing

2	cups mayonnaise
1 1/2	cups chili sauce
1/3	cup minced celery
1/3	cup minced dill pickle
2	Tb lemon juice
1	Tb Worcestershire sauce
1	tsp horseradish sauce

Mix all ingredients well and chill. Traditionally served on wedges of head lettuce, especially iceberg. It is also excellent on Swiss cheese and roast beef sandwiches.

Honey Dressing

1/3	cup honey
1	cup wine vinegar
1	clove garlic, finely chopped
1	cup salad oil

Mix or shake all ingredients in a tightly covered jar and chill. Excellent on spinach greens.

66 Super Salad Additions

Fresh greens don't require a lot of extras because they are so good plain. They can just be combined with each other — different textures, colors and flavors — and taste wonderful. There are traditionalists, who shudder at the thought of sullying their salads with anything not green, but I like the occasional addition. So here, in alphabetical order, is my offering of everything I could think of that can be added to a salad. Some are good in combination; some are good alone. How much you use depends on your mood, the rest of the meal and what you happen to have on hand.

Anchovies	Curry powder	Peppers —
Apple chunks	Dill	green or red
Avocado	Feta cheese	Pickles
Bacon	Eggs	Pimiento
Basil	Garlic	Pine nuts
Bean sprouts	Grapes — green	Radishes
Beets and	or purple	Roquefort
beet greens	Green onions	cheese
Bermuda	Ham	Salami
onion slices	Horseradish	Salmon
Bleu cheese	Kidney beans	Sardines
Capers	Leeks	Shallots
Carrots	Lobster	Shrimp
Carrot curls	Marjoram	Snap beans
Cauliflowerets	Mayonnaise	Snow pea pods
Celery	Mint	Spinach
Chervil	Mushrooms	Sunflower
Chicken bits	Nasturtium leaves,	seeds
Chives	flowers	Swiss chard
Cottage cheese	Nut meats	Swiss cheese
Crabmeat	Olives — ripe or	Tarragon
Cress	green	Tomatoes
Croutons	Parmesan cheese	Tongue
Cucumber	Parsley	Tuna fish
slices	Pearl onions	Turkey bits

Vegetables à la Grecque

Certain vegetables simmered in an aromatic broth and then chilled are wonderful and special accompaniments to a salad, especially if you serve the salad as the first course.

These vegetables are best suited for à la Grecque preparation. Use them separately or combine a few.

Artichoke	Celery hearts or	Pearl onions
hearts	stalks	Peeled eggplant
Asparagus	Green beans	fingers
Carrots	Leeks	Whole green onions
Cauliflowerets	Mushrooms	Zucchini slices

The broth for 4 cups of vegetables:

- 2 cups water
- 1/4 cup olive oil
- 1 garlic clove, crushed
- 1/2 tsp salt
- 1/3 cup lemon juice
- 2 Tb minced green onions or shallots
- 1/4 cup dry white wine
- 2 Tb chopped parsley
- 1 small celery stalk
- pinches of thyme, tarragon
- 1 bay leaf
- 6 black peppercorns

Simmer all ingredients for 10 minutes in a covered saucepan. Add selected vegetables and simmer until barely tender. Do not overcook! Because various vegetables have different cooking times, add the longest-cooking first. Set the timer, and add shorter-cooking ones later to have them all finish together.

Remove vegetables with slotted spoon and put in separate bowl. Boil down broth until there is only about 1/3 cup. Strain it over vegetables and allow to cool. If refrigerated, the vegetables will keep for a few days, but they may be served in a salad as soon as they have cooled.

Spinach

Although a lot of people don't agree with me, I love spinach! It's got to be cooked right, though. Overcooked, I think it's mushy, slimy and bitterly metallic. Cooked gently, it has a distinct flavor, which I think is a wonderful accompaniment to fish, eggs, chicken, roasts or as a separate course in quiche or soufflé and raw as a salad. One pound of fresh spinach cooks down to about one cup, and that is almost enough for two people.

Spinach, like other greens, must be washed well. To serve it plain, just leave the water of the last washing on the leaves, and put the spinach in a large enamel, Pyrex or stainless steel pot.

Or use a steamer that has an inner container full of holes that sits over, not in, about 2 inches of boiling water in the outer container. Cover and cook over low to medium heat. In a few minutes, the spinach will be tender, tasty and ready to serve. Some people like to add vinegar. I prefer salt, pepper and butter, and occasionally a sprinkling of nutmeg.

Precooked, chopped spinach is tasty baked in cream sauce, cheese sauce or with grated Swiss cheese and topped with bread crumbs.

Easy Cream of Spinach Soup

- 1 lb (3 cups) chopped spinach or chard
- ¼ cup chopped onion
- ¼ cup margarine or butter
- 3 Tb flour
- salt and pepper to taste
- 3 cups milk

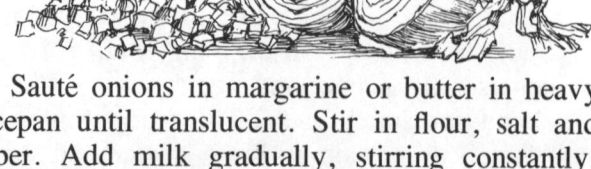

Sauté onions in margarine or butter in heavy saucepan until translucent. Stir in flour, salt and pepper. Add milk gradually, stirring constantly. Cook over low heat to boiling. Simmer and stir for one minute.

Steam well-washed, chopped spinach or chard until it is just tender. Add to cream sauce base and serve.

Spinach Ring

- 2 Tb margarine or butter

3 Tb finely chopped onions
2 cans cream of mushroom soup
3 cups cooked spinach or chard, chopped
1/2 cup bread crumbs
salt and pepper to taste
nutmeg to taste
2 eggs, separated

Preheat oven to 375°. Sauté onions in margarine or butter until tender. Heat the soup, undiluted, stirring until smooth. Add the onions and margarine, spinach, bread crumbs, salt, pepper and nutmeg.

Beat egg yolks until thick. Stir the egg yolks into spinach mixture, very slowly. Set aside. Beat egg white until stiff but not dry. Fold into spinach mixture and pour into buttered ring mold. Set the mold in a pan of hot water and bake 45 minutes or until set. Unmold and serve hot. Very good with baked or roast chicken. Serves 6.

Popeye Burgers

2 lbs raw spinach, chopped
2 lbs ground beef
1/2 cup bread crumbs
1/2 cup shredded Cheddar cheese
2 Tb Worcestershire sauce
1 egg, slightly beaten
1 garlic clove, finely minced
salt and pepper to taste
2 Tb oil or margarine

Mix all ingredients well. Shape into 8 patties and cook in oil in large fry pan over medium heat until desired doneness. Turn only once. The patties may also be broiled. May be served on bread, hard rolls or just plain with mashed potatoes. Serves 4.

Lamb and spinach stew

2 Tb flour
2 lbs boneless lamb stew meat
2 medium onions, chopped
1 1/2 cups stock or bouillon
1 bay leaf
3 lbs fresh spinach, well-washed and chopped
3 cups diced tomatoes
1 tsp salt
1/2 tsp dried rosemary
1/2 tsp freshly ground black pepper
2 Tb flour
2 Tb butter

Dredge cubed stew meat in flour and brown in Dutch oven. Drain fat, leaving only about 1 Tb. Add onions and cook until they are translucent. Add stock and simmer, covered, until tender, about one hour. Add spinach, tomatoes, salt, rosemary and pepper and cook for about 10 minutes or until

spinach is wilted. Blend additional flour with butter and add gradually to stew to thicken. Stir constantly and cook for additional minute. Serve with rice. Serves 6.

Spinach/Noodle Casserole

1 pound noodles
1 1/2 pounds fresh spinach, well-washed
1 Tb lemon juice
3 Tb butter
1 Tb finely chopped onion
1 garlic clove, finely minced
3 Tb flour
1 cup light cream or milk
salt and pepper to taste
pinch of nutmeg
1/2 cup finely chopped ham
1/2 cup buttered soft fresh bread crumbs

Preheat oven to 350°. Cook noodles until just tender and drain. Wilt spinach and chop finely. Add lemon juice. Sauté onion and garlic in butter. Add flour and gradually stir in cream or milk over gentle heat. Season with salt, pepper and nutmeg. Add spinach and stir well. Add noodles and ham and place in shallow, buttered baking dish. Top with crumbs and bake for 20 minutes or until lightly browned.

Celery

Somewhere I heard that you burn more calories eating raw celery than you consume. That may be the reason celery is on almost every diet invented. But it also tastes good and has an appealing texture that helps you to think you are eating something far more substantial. Celery also has a wonderful flavor for soups, stews and salads that makes it an indispensable vegetable.

To prepare raw celery, wash it well, cut it into uniform strips, and eat it plain or serve it with a dip. It can also be filled with a mixture of bleu cheese and heavy cream.

To keep celery crisp, simply stick the stalks in ice water in the refrigerator, and they'll stay for days.

To boil celery, slice washed stalks crosswise into 1-inch slices. Boil it gently in salted water until crispy-tender. It can be served plain with butter or in cream sauce or Hollandaise.

Braised Celery

Wash enough stalks to make 4 per person served. If they are very large, cut in half. Place in a lidded sauté pan and sauté in clarified butter for 2 minutes. Add salt and pepper and barely cover with hot chicken or veal stock. Cover and simmer until tender; remove the stalks to individual serving plates and keep warm in oven. Reduce the stock by at least half. Add again as much heavy cream and bring to a boil, stirring constantly. Add 1/4 to 1/2 cup shredded mild cheese and stir until thickened. Pour some sauce over each serving, and top with an ''X'' of pimiento.

Curried Celery

Cut one whole (large) bunch, or two small ones, into bite-sized pieces crossways. Pare, core and dice 1 large apple; peel and dice one medium onion. Melt chicken fat or lard (or substitute oil & butter) to the point of fragrance, and add the vegetables. Cook and stir until just barely beginning to brown. Turn down the heat and add 1 cup of stock (or bouillon) mixed with 1 Tb cornstarch, 1 tsp (or more) curry powder, 2 tsp capers, a pinch of ground ginger, salt and pepper. Cook over low heat, stirring regularly, until thickened and tender.

Greens

One-dish Supper

All greens are delicious cooked with salt pork.

4 lbs greens (beets, chard, spinach, turnip, mustard)
1/2 lb salt pork
8 small potatoes

Slice salt pork down to the rind. Cover and simmer in sufficient water 1 1/2 hours. Wash greens in several changes of water. Add potatoes and well-washed greens to salt pork and cook until potatoes are tender — about 30 additional minutes.
Serves 4 to 6.

Cornmeal dumplings

An excellent accompaniment for the one-dish supper!

1 cup flour
1/2 tsp salt
2 tsp baking powder
1 cup cornmeal
1 beaten egg
2/3 cup milk

Sift flour, salt, baking powder. Add cornmeal and beaten egg and milk. Stir well but do not beat.
Drop the dumplings on top of the boiling greens and potatoes by spoonfuls. Cover and cook 15 minutes.

Egg Sauce

A nice accompaniment for hot cooked greens, especially beet greens, spinach, chard and kale.

1 hard-boiled egg, chopped
1/4 tsp salt
2 slices bacon, cooked and crumbled
2 Tb mayonnaise
1/2 tsp grated onion

Mix all ingredients together and serve on hot greens.

Collards and Mashed Potatoes

Cook the collards and potatoes in separate pans with water. Drain both. Chop the collards finely and mix with the mashed potatoes. Put in a baking dish in a 400° oven, dot with butter and bake until browned.

Endive Quiche

Quiche is nothing more, really, than scrambled egg pie with extras thrown in, but it tastes special.

8″ partially baked pie shell
4 cups raw, chopped Belgian endive (or spinach, chard or other cooked greens)
2 Tb butter or margarine
1/4 tsp salt
2 Tb water
1 tsp lemon juice
1 1/2 cups whipping cream
3 eggs
pinch of mace
freshly ground black pepper
1/4 cup grated Swiss cheese
1 Tb butter or margarine

Preheat oven to 325°. Place endive in 2-quart, buttered baking dish. Mix salt, water and lemon juice together and pour over endive. Cut a piece of brown paper the same size as the top of the baking dish, butter it and place it on top of the endive. Cover the dish and braise the endive in the oven for 20 to 30 minutes, or until tender.
While the endive is cooking, beat eggs until thick and beat in cream, mace and pepper. Remove endive from oven and drain. Turn oven up to 375°.
Fold endive into egg mixture, pour into pastry shell and sprinkle with cheese and dot with butter.

Bake in upper part of oven for 25 to 30 minutes or until set. Serves 4 to 6.

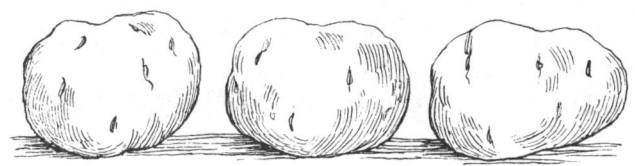

Simple Watercress Soup

1	lb peeled, diced potatoes
1	lb peeled, sliced onions
1 1/2	qts water or chicken stock or broth
1	Tb salt
1/4	lb watercress
2	Tb butter
2	Tb whipping cream
	salt and pepper to taste

Simmer the potatoes and onions together in water with salt until tender. Liquefy in blender or food processor. Chop watercress finely and add to soup. Simmer for 5 minutes. Add salt and pepper. Remove from heat and add butter and cream and serve. Decorate with chopped parsley or chives. May be served hot or cold. Serves 6 to 8.

Stir-Fried Kale

8	cups fresh kale
4	Tb vegetable oil
	salt and pepper to taste

Wash green part of kale leaves and drain.

Heat heavy skillet, electric fry pan or wok and add oil. When the oil is almost smoking, put in the kale. Toss and stir until it is wilted completely. Stir and cook another 5 minutes. Great served with chicken fricassee. Serves 4.

Wilted Lettuce

6	slices of bacon
1/3	cup mild vinegar
	salt and pepper to taste
2	medium heads Boston lettuce or
1	medium head Cos or
	equivalent leaf lettuce

Wash lettuce well and tear into bite-size bits. Fry bacon until crisp. Remove bacon from pan and crumble. To fat in frying pan, add vinegar, salt and pepper. When the mixture boils, add the greens and stir until they are just wilted. Serve hot with bacon crumbles on top. Serves 4.

Dandelion Greens

Most people who eat dandelion greens don't plant them. They just pick them wild early in the spring in meadows and pastures — or on their own lawns.

Well-washed, young dandelion greens are very tasty served raw with sour cream.

If you want to serve cooked dandelion greens, wash them well in several changes of water. Put them in a large pot and cover with boiling water and simmer for 5 minutes. Drain and add fresh boiling water to them and cook until tender. Drain again and serve hot with butter or margarine or vinegar and salt and pepper to taste. If you like a more tangy flavor, cook them in just one water until tender.

CANNING GREENS

Personally, I think greens should just barely be wilted for best taste. If they're cooked for much longer, I think they become bitter. Overcooking, I think, accounts for many people's — especially children's — dislike of greens.

To can greens safely, they must be cooked a long time. For that reason, I am not a great fan of canning them. However, they work well in soups and casseroles. So, if you want to do it — and I put up at least a few quarts every year — here's how:

1. For safety and health, it is important to be careful canning, and the first requirement is to use a pressure canner with an accurate gauge for canning all greens.

For complete instructions and precautions for pressure canning, please carefully read and follow the instruction booklets that accompany your canner and your jars. For additional canning information, write the U.S. Department of Agriculture, Washington, D.C. 20240 and ask them for *Home and Garden Bulletin* No. 8, *Home Canning of Fruits and Vegetables*. You have already paid for it with your tax dollars, so no additional money is required.

2. Assemble all utensils: Pressure canner, Mason jars, lids, bands, tongs or jar lifter, timer, cooling racks, wide-mouth funnel, slotted spoon, wooden or plastic spatula or "bubbler," colander.

Use only Mason jars for home canning. These self-sealing, air-tight jars are safe for canning, because the glass is heat-tempered, which is especially important for pressure canning.

3. Examine and clean all equipment. Check all bands for rust, dents or nicks and jars for chips and cracks.

Wash all equipment in hot, soapy water, but do not immerse top of pressure canner in water — just wipe it with a clean, damp cloth.

Keep clean jars and screw tops hot. Keep dome lids in hot water until ready to use.

4. Prepare freshest, cleanest greens possible. Use freshly picked, tender greens and remove stems and imperfect leaves. Wash greens thoroughly in several changes of water, lifting the greens out and letting the grit settle to the bottom.

5. Greens must be processed hot pack (precooked). Steam (in just enough water to prevent sticking, or use steamer) about 2 1/2 pounds of greens until thoroughly wilted. To hasten wilting and prevent overcooking, turn greens over when steam begins to rise around edges of pan. Cut through greens with sharp knife, pack the greens in hot jars, leaving about one-inch headspace. Add salt, 1/2 tsp per pint or 1 tsp per quart. Cover with boiling water, retaining 1-inch headspace. Remove air bubbles by running non-metallic spatula around inside jar. Adjust jar lids.

6. Process in pressure canner. Pack only the number of jars your pressure canner can accommodate at one time. Put the canner on the burner, and put the jars on the rack in the canner. Add 2 inches of boiling water to the canner. Allow enough space between the jars and the sides of the pot so that the steam can flow freely. Clamp the lid securely.

Leave the valve or petcock open, and set the canner over high heat until steam has escaped for 10 minutes. Then close the petcock or put on the weighted gauge, and let the pressure rise to 10 pounds. Start timing and keep adjusting the heat so that the pressure remains constant. If the pressure drops below 10 pounds, the processing time must be started again.

Processing Time

Pints	70 minutes
Quarts	90 minutes

Your canner instructions may differ with the times given above. If so, follow your canner instructions.

Altitude affects pressure canners. You need to use more pressure and longer cooking time the higher you go.

Feet above sea level	Increase pressure	Increase cooking time
1,000		2 minutes
2,000	to 11 pounds	4 minutes
3,000		6 minutes
4,000	to 12 pounds	8 minutes
5,000		10 minutes

If using a weight control canner, increase pressure to 15 pounds at elevations higher than 2,000 feet.

Do not skimp on processing time!

7. After processing time is completed, turn off heat and wait until pressure has dropped to zero before opening canner. Using tongs or jar lifter, remove the jars and place them upright on a rack or thick towel in a draft-free area, allowing enough room between jars, so air may circulate freely. Do not tighten the rims on the dome lids; you may break the seals.

8. There are three tests for checking the seal on a dome lid.

1) As the vacuum forms, the lid pulls down into the jar and makes a kerplunking sound.

2) After cooling, the lid will be dished in the middle and should stay that way as long as the vacuum is present. You can feel it.

3) After cooling, press the top of the lid with your thumb. If it makes a clicking sound, the seal is *not* complete.

If you find some jars with incomplete seals, put the jars in the refrigerator, and use the food soon. The greens are perfectly good to eat because they are so fresh and you have just cooked them. They just won't hold in storage with imperfect seals.

9. Wipe the jars with a clean, damp cloth and remove the screw bands for re-use. Label the produce clearly, including the date. Store in a cool, dark, dry area.

10. Before serving, reheat all greens by boiling them in an open kettle for 15 minutes. If they smell "off" or if the color or appearance doesn't look right, just dispose of them carefully.

FREEZING GREENS

Frozen greens can often be substituted with success in recipes calling for fresh greens. They aren't quite as good, but they sure are better than nothing or using commercially frozen or canned varieties.

As about two pounds of greens reduce to 10 ounces when wilted, it's easy to realize that you'll need a whole "mess o' greens" in order to have some to freeze plus enough to eat fresh. So if you like greens, just know that it's difficult to plant too much.

For best freezing results, follow these simple steps:

1. Select young, tender leaves. Remove tough stems and imperfect leaves. You may chop them into smaller pieces if you wish.

2. Wash greens thoroughly in several changes of water. Swish them around in a basin of water, and lift them out to drain. The grit will sink to the bottom.

3. Blanch greens in a kettle of boiling water. Almost all greens (beet, chard, kale, mustard, New Zealand and regular spinach and turnip) require 2 minutes blanching. The one exception is collards, and they should be blanched for 3 minutes. If the leaves are very tender, blanch for only 1 1/2 minutes.

4. Chill greens immediately in ice water to stop cooking process and to retain color. Chill for the same amount of time as they were cooked. Don't let them sit around in the water because they will lose flavor.

5. Drain greens well and pack in containers leaving 1/2-inch headspace. Seal, label with contents and date and freeze.

If you've enjoyed this Gardens for All vegetable guide...
we have a whole series of vegetable gardening guides waiting just for you!

Each of the other 10 books in our series covers another favorite vegetable, and is packed with the same from-seed-to-table how-to: planning tips, growing hints, harvesting and preservation, delicious recipes too!

What are *your* family's favorite vegetables? Choose the books that fit *your* vegetable checklist. Or take advantage of our special offer and get the whole set for *complete* vegetable gardening know-how.

Which of these vegetable guides do you need?

Onions
Tomatoes
Beans
Root Crops
Lettuce & Greens
Cucumbers, Melons and Squash
Potatoes
Broccoli, Cauliflower and Cabbage
Eggplants, Peppers and Okra
Corn
Peas and Peanuts
Complete Garden Guide Library

Complete your GFA Garden Library with this special offer!

One at a time	$2.50
3 or more books	$2.00 each
All 11 books	$15.00

"The publications—both the newspaper and the brochures on tomatoes and lettuce—are really impressive—so good! And I am so glad I joined!"
Nancy Eberle, Galena, Illinois

Order Form

Quantity	Title	Price	Total

4th Class shipping, handling & guaranteed delivery. (Allow 4-6 weeks)

Orders to $15	. . . . .add $2	$50.01-$100	. . . . .add $6
$15.01-$25	. . . . .add $3	$100.01 and up	. . . . .add $7
$25.01-$50	. . . . .add $4		

Shipping	
Add'l. 1st Class	
Membership	
Total Due	

For *FASTER* service, please add $2/book for **1st Class.**
GFA Garden Library — add $2 for any number of Guides through a full set.

Please enroll me as a Member of GFA, and send my first issue of
Gardens for All. (Membership dues/subscription $15)

Name _____

Address _____

City _____ State _____ Zip _____

Please send this order form, along with your payment to:
Gardens for All, Dept. C-2, 180 Flynn Avenue, Burlington, VT 05401